Table of Contents

About the Author

Lucius Joseph is President of a non profit organization "Essentials of Life Ministry Inc." established in the Island of Saint Lucia in the West Indies, and the Founding Pastor of a non denominational congregation.

My passion and desire is to help sensitized others of the new birth we all have in the spirit, when we were begotten by Jesus Christ at his resurrection, and how practical and literal is this life in the spirit, which exist simultaneously with the life in the flesh, and are at odds with each other, so that the individual can not do what he/she wants

It is my desire also to help raise our consciousness of God's divine power which has granted to us all things that pertain to life and godliness, through the knowledge of him who called us to his own glory and excellence; by which he has granted to us his precious and very great promises, that through these we may escape from the corruption that is in the world because of passion, and become partakers of the divine nature.

Because, developing the divine nature of Jesus Christ should be our main objective in this life, so that as he is so are we in this world.

Chapter one
Man's Duality

Man is a complex being. His richness and complexity distinguish him from all other living being. The bible for example refers to man as:-

An old man: as well as a new man.

An outward man: and an inward man.

A being who lives in accordance to the flesh: and a being who lives in accordance to the Spirit.

A being with a carnal mind: and a being with a spiritual mind.

Man is so complex he cannot understand his own actions. The Apostle Paul alluded to this fact by saying; "For what I am doing, I do not understand. For what I will to do, that I do not practice; but what I hate, that I do. If then, I do what I will not to do, I agree with the law that it is good.'

"But now, it is no longer I who do it, but sin that dwells in me. For I know that in me (that is, in my flesh) nothing good dwells; for to will is present with me, but how to perform what is good I do not find. For the good that I will to do, I do not do; but the evil I will not to do, that I practice. Now if I do what I will not to do, it is no longer I who do it, but sin that dwells in me" (Romans 7:15-20).

From all indications, there are two diametrically opposite sides of a man, both with their individual characteristics, each tree bearing its own fruit.

To understand man's actions, it is imperative that we understand man's duality.

The Old Man

The old man is the sinful nature that we all inherited from the first Adam, which according to the word of God in Jeremiah chapter seventeen and verse nine, " The heart is deceitful above all things and desperately wicked who can know it?" This sinful powerful nature which is called **SIN**, resides in the flesh in the five physical senses of sight, hearing, smelling, taste, and feelings.

It was crucified with Jesus Christ at His death, so that the body of sin might be done away with, and that we should no longer be slaves of sin. The acts of this sinful nature are obvious, when for example one Lie, cheats, commits adultery, fornication, homosexuality, murder, witchcraft, hatred, discord, jealousy, fits of rage, selfish ambitions, dissensions, fractions, envy, drunkenness, orgies and the like, they are exhibiting the heart and core of that sinful nature.

Carnally Minded

To be carnally minded is to have one's mind occupied with the physical mundane things of the earth. It is a mind that is enmity against God, and which is not subject to the law of God, neither can it ever be; and the end result of such a mind is death.

The admonition is to, Put to death, whatever belongs to this earthly nature, for because of these, the wrath of God is coming, and those who like this will not inherit the kingdom of God.

The Outward Man

The outward man is the physical body which was created from the dust of the ground, and will return to dust. According to Job chapter fourteen, verses one and two; "Man born of woman is of few days and full of trouble. He springs up like a flower and withers away; like a fleeting shadow, he does not endure."

The members of the body are instruments of the soul—the living being, and serve as servant to either the life which is in accordance to the flesh, or the life which is in accordance to the Spirit. The solution to this dilemma according the apostle Paul is; "I put this in human terms because you are weak in your natural selves; just as you used to offer the parts of your body in slavery to impurity and to ever-increasing wickedness, so now offer them in slavery to righteousness leading to holiness" (Romans 6:19).

The New Man

The new man is the holy righteous nature we inherited from Jesus Christ the last Adam, when He resurrected from the dead. As it is written; "Blessed be the God and Father of our Lord Jesus Christ, who according to His abundant mercy has begotten us again to a living hope through the resurrection of Jesus Christ from the dead" (1Peter 1:3). According to the book of Acts chapter seventeen verses 28 and 29; "In Him we live and move and have our being', as also some of your own poets have said, "We are also His offspring."

Man therefore is both the offspring of the first and the last Adam. Each tree bears its own fruit. A good tree does not bear bad fruit, nor does a bad tree bear good fruit. A spring cannot send forth fresh water and bitter water from the same opening. A fig tree can not bear olives, neither will a grape vine bear figs. In like manner, the sinful nature of the first Adam can not produce anything good, and the righteous, holy nature of the Last Adam can not produce anything evil.

The fruit produced by the new man is in contrast to the works of the old man. The fruit produce by the new man is; love, joy, peace, long suffering, kindness, goodness, faithfulness, gentleness, self-control etc.

The admonition to those who now live in accordance to the Spirit is; "You used to walk in these ways (according to the flesh), in the life you once lived. But now you must rid yourselves of all such things as these: anger, rage, malice, slander and filthy language from your lips.

"Therefore, as God's chosen people, holy and dearly loved, clothe yourselves with compassion, kindness, humility, gentleness and patience. Bear with each other and forgive whatever grievances you may have against one another. Forgive as the Lord forgave you.'

" And over all these virtues put on love, which binds them all together in perfect unity. Let the peace of Christ rule in your hearts, since as members of one body you were called to peace.'

"And be thankful. Let the word of Christ dwell in you richly as you teach and admonish one another with all wisdom, and as you sing psalms, hymns and spiritual songs with gratitude in your hearts to God. And whatever you do, whether in word or deed, do it all in the name of the Lord Jesus, giving thanks to God the Father through him" (Colossians 3:7-17).

The Inner /Inward Man

The inward man is the living being who was begotten by the Last Adam the life giving Spirit, it is eternal, and even though the outward man is perishing, yet the inner man is being renewed day by day.

Many people have not come to the realization and knowledge of the fact that there is a life in accordance to the flesh, and one in accordance to the Spirit. These two walks of life are contrary to each other, so that you the individual do not do the things that you wish.

So strong is this battle, not even a rigid set of rules, or a holy, just and good law could protect, or save someone from the walk of the flesh.

The first step towards living in the Spirit is to be born again.

Jesus told Nicodemus, "Truly, truly, I say to you, unless one is born anew [again], he cannot see the kingdom of God" (John 3:3).

This new birth is not a physical birth, but a spiritual one. Jesus further explained to Nicodemus saying, "That which is born of the flesh is flesh, and that which is born of the Spirit is spirit. Do not marvel that I said to you 'You must be born anew'. The wind blows where it wills, and you hear the sound of it, but you do not know whence it comes or whither it goes, so it is with every one who is born of the Spirit" (John 3:6-8).

Physically man is born of water and in water as a fetus within the amniotic sac [water bag]; water is the main source of our physical life. The human body is approximately 65-85 percent water. Water molecules combined with inhaled oxygen produce water in the human body, so basically, human beings are born of water.

The source of life for the life in the flesh is air, water and food. It is strengthen and developed through physical exercises. Similarly the spiritual life also requires a source of sustenance which is diametrically different to that of the physical life.

Before one can be born of the Spirit, he must first be begotten in the Spirit, by a Spirit Being. For this reason, Jesus Christ, the last Adam, the second Man from heaven, who is a life-giving Spirit, begat humanity at His resurrection and gave man life in the Spirit.

Before Jesus Christ came the spirit of man was dead. As it is written; "As for you, you were dead in your transgressions and sins, in which you used to live when you followed the ways of this world and of the ruler of the kingdom of the air, the spirit who is now at work in those who are disobedient (Ephesians 2:1-2).

But Jesus Christ gave life back to the spirit of man, as it is written; "Praise, be to the God and Father of our Lord Jesus Christ! In His great mercy He has given us new birth [begotten] into a living hope through the resurrection of Jesus Christ from the dead, and into an inheritance that can never perish, spoil or fade—kept in heaven for you, who through faith are shielded by God's power until the coming of the salvation that is ready to be revealed in the last time" (1Pet.1:3-5).

This new birth, which is our life in Jesus Christ, is **the living hope we all have in seeing the kingdom**. Because of God's great love for us, God, who is rich in mercy, made us alive with Christ even when we were dead in transgressions—it is by grace we have been saved.—And God raised us up with Christ and seated us with Him in the heavenly realms in Christ Jesus.

Jesus Christ is the Resurrection and the life, he is eternal life. He is the true vine, and we are the branches. In Him therefore we all live and move and have our being.

The testimony or witness that we have from God concerning His Son is that: "God has given us eternal life, and this life is in His Son" (1John. 5:11).

Humanity has been granted this new life in the Spirit so that;

    A. Humanity may come to know God, the only true God, and Jesus Christ, whom God has sent.

    B. They would seek and perhaps reach out for Him and find Him though He is not far from each one of us, For in Him we (all) live and move and have our being.

C. They may see the kingdom of God.

We should know also that, "The Son of God has come and has given us understanding, so that we may know Him who is true. And we are in Him who is true—even in His Son Jesus Christ. He is the true God and eternal life" (1John.5:20).

Eternal life is Jesus Christ, the foundation on which we have to build our immortal body [house] without which no one can inherit the kingdom, because, "Flesh and blood cannot inherit the Kingdom, nor does the perishable inherit the imperishable" (1Corinthians15:50).

Therefore, when Jesus Christ came into the world he said; "The thief comes only to steal and kill and destroy; I have come that they may have life, and have it to the full" (John 10:10).

This life began when humanity became begotten by Jesus Christ at his resurrection, and one begins to live this life when his/her spirit is joined to the spirit of the Lord and become one with him, because it is the Spirit that gives life.

The Spirit therefore is the source of life in the spirit, similarly to the breath of air which gives life to the human body. According to Job chapter 34:14; "If God should take back his spirit to himself, and gather to himself his breath, all flesh would perish together, and man would return to dust." It is when God's Holy Spirit is joined to our human spirit, and we are being led by the Spirit of God, that we become children of God.

Comparatively to the water and food which sustains the life in the flesh, the blood and the flesh of Jesus Christ in the form of the wine and the bread are the necessities for the sustenance of the life in the spirit. For thus says the

Lord; "Do not work for food that spoils, but for food that endures to everlasting life, which the Son of Man will give you" (John 6:27).

The food which the Son of Man gave that sustains the life that he gave, and which endures to everlasting life is his flesh and blood. For thus the Lord says; "I am the living bread that came down from heaven, if anyone eats of this bread, he will live for ever. This bread is my flesh, which I will give for the life of the world."

He continues; "I tell you the truth, unless you can eat the flesh of the Son of Man and drink his blood, you have no life in you. Whoever eats my flesh and drinks my blood has eternal life, and I will raise him up at the last day. For my flesh is real food, and my blood is real drink:'

" Whosoever eats my flesh and drinks my blood remains in me, and I in him. Just as the living Father sent me and I live because of the Father, so the one who feeds on me will live because of me. This is the bread that came down from heaven. Your forefathers ate the manna and died, but he who feeds on this bread will live for ever" (John 6:51-58).

The exercise necessary to strengthened and develop the spiritual life is the exercising of the mind by studying the word of God, and put into action what has been taught. Because we are admonished saying; "Do not lie to one another, seeing that you have put off the old nature with its practices, and have put on the new nature, which is being renewed in knowledge after the image of its Creator" (Colossians 3:9-10).

One must not only be Born again in the Spirit, but must also be Born of the Spirit

To be born of the Spirit, which is to receive immortality, or everlasting life, one must have the Spirit of God living in him/her, For it is written; "If the Spirit of Him who raised Jesus from the dead dwells in you, He who raised Christ Jesus from the dead will give life to your mortal bodies also through His Spirit who dwells in you" (Romans 8:11). Anyone who does not have the Spirit of Christ does not belong to Him.

Without Christ living in us in the person of the Holy Spirit the cycle of our spiritual life is incomplete.

The complete cycle of our spiritual life as stated by Jesus Christ is as follows: "I am in My Father, and you are in me, and I am in you" (John.14:20).He also said, "Believe me when I say that I am in the Father and the Father is in me" (John.14:11).

Although we have new life in the Spirit, or have been born {begotten] again, by having our existence in Christ, we nevertheless must have Christ living in us in the person of the Holy Spirit to guarantee the redemption of our bodies.

Jesus alluded to this by saying, "Abide in Me, and I in you. As a branch cannot bear fruit by itself, unless it abides in the vine, neither can you, unless you abide in me. I am the vine, you are the branches. He who abides in Me, and I in him, he it is that bears much fruit, for apart from Me you can do nothing" (John 15:4-5).

Having been saved by God's grace, and being seated in Christ, or being a branch of the true vine, is not the sum total of our spiritual life. There is the possibility of the branch being cut off by the gardener, who is the Father, if the branch does not bear fruit. Not only must the branch abide in the vine, but Christ must also be in the branch. It is to those who received Him, and believe in His name, He gave the right to become children of God.

And it is only at this point the Father qualifies the individual to share in the inheritance of the saints in the kingdom of light, by rescuing him/her from the dominion of darkness and brought him/her into the kingdom of the Son of His love. Christ in us is our only hope of glory.

Walking in the Spirit

Not only are we to live in the Spirit, but we are also required to walk in the Spirit, which basically means to keep in step with the Spirit which is the word of God. In other words it simply means to, be obedient to the word of God as alluded to by Jesus who said, "It is the Spirit that gives life, the flesh is of no avail, the word that I have spoken to you are spirit and life." (John.6:63).

To walk in the Spirit therefore, is to be led by the Spirit, and allow the Spirit to teach us, and just as He has taught us, we should abide in Him. For we are told; "As for you, the anointing you received from him remains in you, and you do not need anyone to teach you. But as his anointing teaches you about all things and as his anointing is real, not counterfeit…just as he has taught you, remain in him" (1John.2: 27).

Life according to the Spirit

Life in accordance to the Spirit is, living in accordance to the nature of Jesus Christ, the Spirit Man from heaven, who came to set us an example that we should follow His steps, who committed no sin, and no deceit was found in His mouth.

Those who live in the Spirit or in accordance to the nature of Jesus Christ have crucified the sinful nature with all its passions and desires. And since we live by the Spirit, we are to keep in step with the Spirit.

Walking in the Spirit, or living according to the Spirit is simply, "not fulfilling the lust of the flesh". For it is written;

"I say then, Walk in the Spirit and you shall not fulfill the lust of the flesh. For the flesh lusts against the Spirit, and the Spirit against the flesh; and these are contrary to one another, so that you do not do the things that you wish" (Galatians 5:16-17).

Spiritually Minded

Living and walking in the spirit requires that we be spiritually minded, meaning that we are to have a mind which is mindful of the things of God, and not the things of the earth, it is a mind which is subject or obedient to the laws of God, and the end result is life and peace.

Unfortunately, most people are ignorant of the duality of man's life, and do not restraint the old sinful nature which dominates human life. But, of this time of ignorance God has overlooked, but now He commands all people everywhere to repent.

For He has set a day when He will judge the world with justice by the Man He has appointed. He has given proof of this to all men by raising Him from the dead. And, we must all appear before the judgment seat of Christ , that each one may receive what is due to him for the things done while in the body, whether good or bad.

Chapter Two

The Process of Spiritual Growth

Man's duality is symbolic to Abraham's two sons Ishmael and Isaac. Ishmael was born from Hagar a bond woman, and he was born according to the flesh. Signifying that, his birth was orchestrated and carried out by the will and passion of the flesh.

On the other hand, Isaac's birth was from Sarah a free woman and came as the result of Abraham's faith in the promise of God.

Abraham, "Not being weak in faith, did not consider his own body, already dead (since he was about a hundred years old), and the deadness of Sarah's womb. He did not waver at the promise of God through unbelief, but was strengthened in faith, giving glory to God, and being fully convinced that what God had promised, he was also able to perform" (Romans 4:11-12).

The same way Ishmael who was born according to the flesh persecuted Isaac who was born according to the Spirit, even so now, the life in the flesh is opposing and persecuting the life in the Spirit.

Comparing the Life in the Spirit with that of the Flesh

Living in the spirit to some people is something vague and nebulous: they see it as something figurative and not something that is real and literal. We have been told however that, what may be known about God is plain, because God has made it plain. "For since the creation of the world God's invisible qualities...his eternal power and divine nature... have been clearly seen, being understood from what has been made, so that men are without excuse" (Romans 1:20).

Therefore exactly what is seen and known about the life in the flesh, reveals what is taking place in the life in the Spirit. The only difference is that they move in opposite directions, they are in constant conflict with each other, and the end result is in contrast to each other. The comparison between the two natures, are like two different trees and each bearing its own fruit. For example:

Life in the Flesh verses	Life in the Spirit
1. Breath of Air	1. Jesus Christ the life-giving Spirit
2. Water	2. The Blood of Jesus Christ
3.Food	3. The Body of Jesus Christ
4. Exercise	4. Renewing the Mind
5. Sleep and Rest	5. Prayer and Fasting
6. Recreation	6. Rejoice before the Lord
7. The End Result	7. The End Result

1. Life in the flesh as compared to life in the Spirit

Life in the flesh originated from the first Adam who became a living being. As a living being, the life is temporary, it is typical to a charged battery, or a wind up clock which will gradually discharge or wind down until it eventually becomes dead or stop working.

The source of that physical life is the breath of air. According to the apostle James; "…For what is your life? It is even a vapor that appears for a little time and then vanishes away" (James 4:14). And Job likewise said; "Oh, remember that my life is a breath!" (Job 7:7).

The Life in the Spirit on the other hand, originates from Jesus Christ the life-giving Spirit, the last Adam, the second man from heaven who is the resurrection and the life. Unlike the first Adam who became a living being from the dust of the ground, and degenerates until it dies and return to dust, the last Adam became a life-giving spirit, a spirit being who generates life, and increases from one degree of glory to another.

The main objective for Christ's coming to earth is to give life. He said, "…I came that they may have life, and have it abundantly" (John 10:10). And so he gives to all men life and breath and everything. It is in him we live and move and have our existence. He is the vine and we are the branches.

2. Water for the human survival as compared to the real drink for the spiritual life

Water is the second most important necessity to sustain life. According to the World Book Encyclopedia, "Every living thing must keep its water supply near normal, or it will die. A man can live without food for more than a month, but he can live without water for only about a week. If the body loses more than 20 percent of its normal water content, he will die painfully."

Comparatively, the spiritual drink is as important for the spiritual life, because the one who came to bring us the more abundant life says; "Everyone who drinks of this water will thirst again, but whoever drinks of the water that I shall give him will never thirst; the water that I shall give him will become in him a spring of water welling up to everlasting life" (John 4:13-14).

So important is this water to the spiritual life, the Lord says; "Truly, truly, I say to you, unless you eat the flesh of the Son of Man and drink his blood, you have no life in you" (John 6:53).

Water is a necessity for washing, cleaning and removal of stains, in like manner, the spiritual drink is also a necessity for the cleansing and removal of stains, in order to present us holy and blameless and irreproachable before him. For, "In him we have redemption through his blood, the forgiveness of sins, according to the riches of his grace" (Ephesians 1: 7).

3. Food for human survival as compared to the real food for spiritual life

According to the World Book Encyclopedia, "Food is one of our most basic needs, we cannot live without it. Food gives us the energy for everything we do – walking, talking, working, playing, reading, and even thinking and breathing. Food also provides the energy our nerves, muscles, heart, and glands need to work. In addition, food supplies the nourishing substances our bodies require to build and repair tissues and to regulate body organs and systems...Food does more than help keep us alive, strong, and healthy, it also adds pleasure to living."

Food is so important to the physical life, and yet the one who came to give us the more abundant life says; "Do not labor for the food which perishes, but for the food which endures to eternal life, which the Son of Man will give to you; for on him has God the Father set his seal" (John 6:27).

The food which is given to us for our spiritual life is more of a necessity than that of the physical life for thus says the Lord; "I am the living bread which came down from heaven. If anyone eats of this bread, he will live for ever: and the bread that I shall give is my flesh, which I shall give for the life of the world" (John 6:51).

He said again; "Whoever eats my flesh and drinks my blood has eternal life, and I will raise him up at the last day, for my flesh is food indeed, and my blood is drink indeed. He who eats my flesh and drinks my blood abides in me and I in him.

As the living Father sent me, and I live because of the Father, so he who feeds on me will live because of me. This is the bread which came down from heaven – not as your fathers ate the manna, and are dead. He who eats this bread will live for ever" (John 6: 54-58).

4. Exercise for human health and growth as compared to exercise for spiritual health and development

We are told that Physical exercise profits a little. It helps to maintain and improve body functions and posture. It increases muscle tone, strength and endurance. Regular vigorous exercise also increases the efficiency and capacity of the heart and lungs and helps people maintain their proper weight.

Similarly exercising of the mind by studying the word of God is paramount to the development and growth of the new life in the spirit, because, "The new man is being renewed in knowledge according to the image of its Creator", and therefore one has to, "Grow in the grace and in the knowledge of our Lord and Savior Jesus Christ: To whom be the glory both now and forever. Amen" (Colossians 3:10; 2 Peter 3:18).

The apostle Paul's prayer for those who believe in this new life in the spirit is that, "...You may be filled with the knowledge of his will in all spiritual wisdom and understanding, to lead a life worthy of the Lord, fully pleasing to him, bearing fruit in every good work and increasing in the knowledge of God." (Colossians 1:9-10).

5. Rest and Sleep as compared to Prayer and Fasting

According to the World Book Encyclopedia, "Rest and Sleep helps overcome fatigue and restore energy to the body. Everyone needs rest and sleep, but the amount required differs for each individual... Rest and relaxation are as important as sleep. After strenuous work or exercise, a person may need a period of total rest. At other times, only relaxation or a change of pace is necessary…if rest and relaxation do not relieve fatigue and tension, the individual may have a physical or emotional problem."

Similarly the spiritual life encounters fatigue and tension, due to trials and temptations, but instead of rest and sleep as with the physical, one requires prayer and fasting. Jesus Christ is our perfect example in living the life in the Spirit. He did not require spiritual food to sustain him since he himself is the source of life. He did not have to exercise the mind since he himself is the living word, for example;

On one Feast of Tabernacles, halfway through the feast Jesus went to the temple court and began to teach, on hearing him, "The Jews were amazed and asked, "How did this man get such learning without having studied?" Jesus answered, "My teaching is not my own. It comes from him who sent me" (John 7:15-16).

He nevertheless experienced fatigue through trials and temptations, and the way he handled it was by staying in close contact to the Father in order to receive the strength and rejuvenation required. We are told that, "Very early in the morning, while it was still dark, Jesus got up, left the house and went off to a solitary place, where he prayed." He often withdrew to lonely places and prayed.

On one occasion, "Jesus went out to a mountainside to pray, and spent the night praying to God." On the night of his severe trial, "He went as usual to the Mount of Olives, and his disciples followed him. On reaching the place, he said to them, "Pray that you will not fall into temptation." He withdrew himself about a stone's throw beyond them, knelt down and prayed, Father, if you are willing, take this cup from me; yet not my will, but yours be done." And,"An angel from heaven appeared to him and strengthened him, and being in anguish, he prayed more earnestly, and his sweat was like drops of blood falling to the ground. When he rose from prayer and went back to the disciples, he found them asleep, exhausted from sorrow. "Why are you sleeping?" He asked them. Get up and pray so that you will not fall into temptation" (Luke 22:39-46).

6. Recreation for the physical life as compared to the Spiritual life

Recreation is an activity that people voluntarily pursue for personal enjoyment and satisfaction, it provides pleasure for people, and also makes an important contribution to an individual's mental and physical health. Some people find recreation in helping others through volunteer work, and donate their leisure time to such activities as visiting shut-ins, or serve as leaders in their community.

Similarly there are moments of recreation for those who live the life in the spirit. They are instructed saying; "Be sure to set aside a tenth of all that your fields produce each year. Eat the tithe of your grain, new wine and oil, and the first born of your herds and flocks in the presence of the Lord your God at the place he will choose as a dwelling for his name, so that you may learn to revere the Lord your God always.'

"But if the place is too distant and you have been blessed by the Lord your God and cannot carry your tithe (because the place where the Lord will choose to put his name is so far away), then exchange your tithe for silver, and take the silver with you and go to the place the Lord your God will choose. Use the silver to buy whatever you like; cattle, sheep, wine or other fermented drink, or anything you wish.'

"Then you and your household shall eat there in the presence of the Lord your God and rejoice. And do not neglect the

Levites living in your towns, for they have no allotment or inheritance of their own" (Deuteronomy 14:22-27).

7. The End result of the physical life as compared to the End result of the spiritual life

The physical life is a temporary existence which is lived in a physical body that was formed from the dust of the ground. No matter how much time, effort and money spent on it, it degenerates and ultimately returns to dust. For this cause we have been admonished saying; "Do not be deceived: God cannot be mocked. A man reaps what he sows, the one who sows to his own flesh, will from the flesh reap corruption…" (Galatians 6:7-8).

The end result of the life in the spirit is diametrically opposite to that of the flesh, because while the outward man is perishing, the inward man is being renewed day by day, because its source of life is a life-giving Spirit.

The irony of truth is, there is a physical body, and there is also a spiritual body, both are being built and nourished simultaneously, one should not make the mistake of ignoring the existence of any, both need to be provided for, cared for, and develop to their full potential. At the expiration of the temporary physical life, the spiritual body attains its maximum growth and glorification, and those who have sown to the Spirit will of the Spirit reap Everlasting life.

Spiritual life is extracted from Jesus Christ through faith, and it is being sustained and developed by the grace of God, which is defined as God's unmerited favor, and consist of:-

(a) God's favor, which is his great love in giving us his only begotten Son, that whosoever believes in him should not perish but have everlasting life.

(b) His gifts, talents, and abilities, which makes everyone unique, and it is given to the honor and glory of God, therefore, what we are is a gift from God, and what we become is a gift to God.

© His forgiving mercy - the means by which we can have our sins forgiven, in order to maintain our relationship with him.

(d) His Gospel - The good news of salvation, the medium by which we can grow in the grace and knowledge of our Lord and Savior Jesus Christ.

(e) The hope of Everlasting life, as it is written; "...Gird up the loins of your mind, be sober, and rest your hope fully upon the grace that is to be brought to you at the revelation of Jesus Christ" (1Peter 1:13).

The grace of God is the ultimate source of our salvation because according to the book of Acts chapter 15: verse 11, "We believe that through the grace of the Lord Jesus Christ both Jews and Gentiles shall be saved in the same manner."

Grace is also the source of our calling, the source of our faith, the source of our justification, the source of our forgiveness and the source of our consolation. Because we are being justified freely by his grace through the redemption that is in Christ Jesus, for in him we have redemption through his blood, the forgiveness of sins, according to the riches of his grace.

Our spiritual growth begins with the activation of faith in the grace which we have all received according to the measure of Christ's gift.

we are told that, "There is one body and one Spirit, just as we were called to the one hope that belongs to our call, one Lord, one faith, one baptism, one God and Father of us all, who is above all and through all and in all. But grace was given to each of us according to the measure of Christ's gift" (Ephesians 4:4-7).

It is written, "For by grace you have been saved through faith; and this is not our own doing, it is the gift of God - not because of works, lest any man should boast."

Since we are justified by faith, we have peace with God through our Lord Jesus Christ, through whom we have obtained access to this grace in which we stand, and we rejoice in **our hope of sharing the glory of God.**

The faith that is required for salvation is not our faith, but faith in the righteousness of our God and Savior Jesus Christ, who has given us a new nature, created after the likeness of God in true righteousness and holiness

As it is written: "as one man's trespass led to condemnation of all men so one man's act of righteousness leads to acquittal and life for all men.'

"For, as by one man's disobedience many were made sinners; so by one man's obedience many will be made righteous" (Romans 5:18-19).

This is the gospel or good news which, "Those who have heard the word of truth, the gospel of our salvation, and have believed in him, are sealed with the promised Holy Spirit, which is the guarantee of our inheritance until we acquire possession of it, to the praise of his glory" (Ephesians 1:13-14).

And, "As God's divine power has granted us all things that pertain to life and godliness, through the knowledge of him who called us to his own glory and excellence, by which he has granted to us his precious and very great promises, that through these [his divine power and promises} we may escape from the corruption that is in the world because of passion, and **become partakers of the divine nature**" (2 Peter1:3-4).

God's ultimate plan for man is for man to grow in the nature of God, and have dominion over his creation. For from the beginning the Lord said, "Let us make man in our image, after our likeness; and let them have dominion over the fish of the sea, and over the birds of the air, and over the cattle, and over all the earth, and over every creeping thing that creeps upon the earth" (Genesis 1:26).

For this reason we have been admonished saying, "Let no one glory in men. For all things are yours; whether Paul or Apollos or Cephas, or the world or life or death, or things present or things to come - all are ours; and we are Christ's, and Christ is God's" (1Corinthians 3:21-23).

We should at no time lose focus of the main objective of our human life.

We are also admonished saying, "Blessed be the God and Father of our Lord Jesus Christ, who has blessed us in Christ with every spiritual blessing in the heavenly places, even as he chose us in him before the foundation of the world, that we should be holy and blameless before him.

"He destined us in love to be his sons through Jesus Christ, according to the purpose of his will, to the praise of his glorious grace which he freely bestowed on us in [Jesus Christ] the Beloved" (Ephesians 1:3-6).

Spiritual life originates from Jesus Christ who is the resurrection and the life. He is the vine we are the branches.

We extract spiritual life from Christ in whom we stand, but without faith it is impossible to please God, for whoever would draw near to God must believe that he exists and that he rewards those who seek him.

However, faith is insufficient of itself to help us grow in the nature of God, because faith by itself if it has no works is dead. Therefore, faith has to be supplemented with virtue, and virtue with knowledge. Because the new nature is being renewed in knowledge after the image of its Creator; for we all with unveiled face, are beholding the glory of the Lord, and are being transformed into his likeness from one degree of glory to another; for this comes from the Lord who is the Spirit.

Then knowledge because it makes one arrogant, has to be supplemented with temperance or self control, and temperance supplemented with perseverance, in order to have the tenacity to stick to the task ahead.

Perseverance must be supplemented with godliness, which is to live holy lives; And godliness supplemented with brotherly kindness which is to demonstrate the second of the great commandment, which is to love you neighbor as your self, and finally, brotherly kindness supplemented with love which is the very nature of God.

We are told that, "If these things are ours and abound, they will keep us from being ineffective or unfruitful in the knowledge of our Lord Jesus Christ."

On the other hand, "Whoever lacks these things is blind and shortsighted and has forgotten that he was cleansed from his old sins."

We are admonished therefore to, "Be the more zealous to confirm your call and election, for if you do this you will never fall: so there will be richly provided for you an entrance into the eternal kingdom of our Lord and Savior Jesus Christ" (2 Peter. 1:10-11).

It is imperative that we all know these things, because faith comes from what is heard, and what is heard comes by the preaching of Christ.

But how are men to call upon him in whom they have not believed? And how are they to believe in him of whom they have never heard? And how are they to hear without a preacher? And how can men preach unless they are sent?

Glorious Everlasting Life

Everlasting life is the reward one receives for sowing to the Spirit, as it is written; "Do not be deceived, God is not mocked; for whatever a man sows, that he will also reap. For he who sows to his flesh will of the flesh reap corruption, but he who sows to the Spirit will of the Spirit reap everlasting life" (Galatians 6:7-8).

So what exactly is Everlasting life? Is it the same as eternal life?

Unfortunately not too many people know the difference between the two. The reason for that it is because man does not know his true identity.

Man is spirit in a physical body.

Since the death and resurrection of Jesus Christ the last Adam, the Spirit Man from heaven, mankind is no more regarded according to the flesh. Because at the death of Jesus Christ, humanity was buried with Him, and at His resurrection humanity became a new creation, a spirit being begotten of the last Adam, the life-giving Spirit who is the resurrection and the life; and who gives life to everyone who comes into the world.

Humanity was dead in trespasses and sins, but was made alive together with Christ, and made to sit together in the heavenly places in Christ Jesus, who gives to all life, breath, and all things, so that they should seek the Lord in the hope that they might grope for Him and find Him, though He is not far from each one of us; For in Him we live and move and have our being [existence]. We are also His offspring. He is the Vine and we are the branches.

It is made abundantly clear that, no one can come to Christ, unless the Father who sent Christ draws him. In like manner, no one comes to the Father except through Jesus Christ who is the way, the truth, and the life. Therefore, the Father drew all men to Christ on the cross, in order that they can seek Him, and find Him, through belief and acceptance of the death and resurrection of Jesus Christ.

The same way mankind inherited the sinful nature of the first Adam in his flesh, he also has inherited the nature of the Last Adam [Jesus Christ] in his spirit. For it is written; "As through one man's offence judgment came to all men, resulting in condemnation, even so through one man's righteous act **the free gift [eternal life - Jesus Christ]** came to **all men**, resulting in justification of life." And, "As by one man's disobedience many were made sinners: so also by one man's obedience many will be made righteous" (Romans 5:17-19).

Mankind received the gift of eternal life at the resurrection of Jesus Christ, when they were begotten by him, and this gives everyone the equal opportunity to see the kingdom of God, but this new life will not necessarily grant anyone entry into the kingdom of God, because the complete cycle is, Christ is in the Father, Mankind is in Christ, but mankind has to choose on his own volition to have Christ in them, and unless Christ is in us there is no hope, for Christ in us is the hope of glory. "Truly these times of ignorance God has overlooked, and now he commands all men everywhere to repent" (Acts 17:30).

Eternal Salvation

The life which mankind has standing in Jesus Christ is spiritual and eternal. But when one believes and receives Jesus Christ as Lord and Savior, he receives the right or authority to become a child of God, an adopted son. He is then translated from the kingdom of darkness, into the kingdom of the Son of God's love.

At the point of acceptance, and translation from the kingdom of darkness into the kingdom of light, the individual receives eternal salvation. "Christ gives them eternal life, and they shall never perish; neither shall anyone snatch them out of His hand (John 10:28-29).

Eternal Salvation is to believe and accept what transpired on the cross. It is to believe in Jesus Christ as the Beloved Son of God who divested Himself of His glory to become the Son of Man, so that, "As Moses lifted up the serpent in the wilderness, even so must the Son of man be lifted up, that whoever believes in Him may have eternal life" (John 3:14-15).

Those who choose to believe Christ and receive Him have already been born again, "Not of blood [human life], nor of the will of the flesh [human passion and desires], nor of the will of man [one's determination], but of God" (John 1:12-13).

It is, by grace we have all been saved through faith and that not of ourselves, it is **the gift of God**, not of works lest anyone should boast. Eternal life is Jesus Christ, who is also the substance of faith, he is God's gift to all mankind, and in whom we all stand.

Eternal Life therefore means two things:-

- Eternal existence of the spirit:

- Eternal salvation of the spirit

Everlasting Life

Everlasting life however is different from both the eternal existence of the spirit, and the eternal salvation of the spirit. It is the everlasting existence of the human body, which has a beginning and would have naturally ended, for it is appointed unto man to die, but it will be made to live for ever. In contrast, eternal life has eternally existed, and will continue to exist for ever. Eternal death is not the cessation of life as with physical death, but it is separation from God.

Everlasting life therefore, is the immortality of the human body which Christ alluded to in John 3:5, stating, "Most assuredly I say to you, unless one is of born of water [flesh] and the Spirit, he cannot enter the kingdom of God."

In order for anyone to inherit the kingdom of God, the mortal must put on immortality, and the corruptible must put on incorruption, because Flesh and blood cannot inherit the kingdom of God: nor does corruption inherit incorruption.

Everlasting life or immortality is guaranteed only to those who, not only believe in Jesus Christ as the Beloved Son of God, who became the Son of Man, but who also believes in Jesus Christ as the Begotten Son of God.

While eternal life is a gift, everlasting life however is a reward for righteous living, which leads to holiness, and at the end one reaps the reward of everlasting life. For it is written; "Now that you have been set free from sin, and have become slaves to God, the benefit you reap leads to holiness, and the result is everlasting life." Whereas eternal life is a free gift, for the wages of sin is death, but the gift of God is eternal life in Jesus Christ our Lord" (Romans 6:22-23).

It is those who believe in Jesus Christ as the begotten Son of God, and who walks as Jesus Christ walked that should not perish but have everlasting life.

The truth of the matter is Christ became the begotten Son of God at the resurrection when He was; "Declared to be the Son of God with power, according to the Spirit of holiness" (Romans 1:4).

As God alone, Christ could not have saved us, because He cannot die. As man alone He could not saved us either, for he could have only saved Himself. He had to be both God and man.

As the Son of Man, Jesus Christ was made lower than the angels for the suffering of death, but as the begotten Son of God, He is crowned with glory and honor. "For to which of the angels did God ever say; 'You are My Son, today I have begotten you? And again, 'I will be to Him a Father, and he shall be to me a Son? But when He again brings the first born [from mortal to immortal] into the world, He says; let the angels of God worship Him" (Hebrews 1:5-6)

The Son of Man became the Begotten Son of God by the quality of life He lived as the Son of Man, and this life is indicative of how His followers ought to live.

Jesus Christ is the only begotten Son of the Father, but became the first born [from mortal to immortal] among many brethren who will receive the adoption as sons.

The life that he lived, which we ought to follow in order to receive everlasting life is a life of:-

• Holiness [separation from sin]: for we are admonished to, "Be holy for I am holy."

• Loving righteousness, which is being obedient to his word, for, "He who practices righteousness is righteous just as He is righteous."

• Hating lawlessness, meaning, hating disobeying the laws of God.

• Being obedient to the Father which is being obedient to every word of God.

• Humility as we are admonished to, "Let this mind be in you which was also in Christ Jesus.: who being in very nature God, did not consider equality with God something to be grasped, but made himself nothing, taking the very nature of a servant, being made in human likeness. And being found in appearance as a man, he humbled himself and became obedient to death – even death on a cross" (Philippians 2: 5-8)!

• Being completely dependent upon the Father, as Jesus said; I tell you the truth, the Son can do nothing by himself." And, "By myself I can do nothing" (John 5:19, 30).

• Being led by the Holy Spirit, because it is those who are led by the Spirit are the sons of God.

• Love being the motivating factor for all His works; as it is written; "God is love. Whoever lives in love lives in God, and God in him: In this way, love is made complete among us so that we will have confidence on the Day of Judgment, because in this world we are like him" (1John 4:16-17).

• Being an over-comer: because, it is those who overcome will be granted to sit with him on his throne, even as he himself overcame, and sat down with his Father on his throne.

This is the criterion for everlasting life, the immortality of the body, which is our eternal inheritance, which unfortunately some will forfeit. For, it is written; "Each one's work will become manifest; for the day will declare it, because it will be revealed by fire; and the fire will test each one's work, of what sort it is. If anyone's work which he has built on Christ [eternal life] endures, he will receive a reward. If anyone's work is burned, he will suffer loss; but he himself [spirit man] will be saved, yet so as through fire" (1Corinthians 3:13-15).

The structure we are building is developing the nature [character] of Jesus Christ. Hence, the degree of glory is dependent on how much we have come to the unity of the faith and the knowledge of the Son of God, to a perfect man, to the measure of the stature of the fullness of Christ. For, as we behold His glory we are being transformed into the same image, from glory to glory just as by the Spirit of the Lord.

Receiving the free gift of eternal life, and being saved is not the ultimatum, this is only the foundation or the access by which we can come to know the one and only true God, and Jesus Christ whom God has sent. In addition to these one has to seek honor, glory, and immortality.

One has to allow Jesus Christ to be formed in them and be involved in the construction of the spiritual temple, which is our eternal inheritance.

Measuring our Spiritual growth

How can our spiritual growth be measured? Is it possible to measure it as we are able to measure our physical growth?

We are told that, "God's divine power has granted to us all things that pertain to life and godliness, through the knowledge of Him who called us to His own glory and excellence [virtue], by which he has granted to us His precious and very great promises, that through these we may escape from the corruption that is in the world because of passion, and become partakers of the divine nature" (2 Peter 1:2-4)..

The objective for human life is to develop God's divine nature and having Christ formed in us. It is to rid the body of sin, so that the body can become the spiritual temple of God, and our everlasting dwelling.

The growth and development of the new spirit man is, "In knowledge after the image of its Creator" And therefore we are admonished to, "Grow in grace and in the knowledge of our Lord and Savior Jesus Christ" (Colossians3:10; 2 Peter 3:18).

All of God's promises to us are to His praise and glory. They are all contained in the glory and virtue [excellence] of Jesus Christ which we are to emulate and share, "For no matter how many promises God has made, they are "Yes" in Christ. And so through Him the "Amen" is spoken by us to the glory of God" (2Corinthians 1:20).

Therefore, because of God's promises, "We are to purify ourselves from everything that contaminates body and spirit, perfecting holiness out of reverence for God" (2 Corinthians 7:1).

In order to be able to measure our spiritual development, we need to clearly define what is glory and virtue. We ought not to be afraid of examining ourselves. In fact, the exhortation is to, "Examine yourselves as to whether you are in the faith. Prove yourselves. Do you not know yourselves; that Jesus Christ is in you? - Unless you are disqualified" (2Corinthians 13:5-6).

The state of Glory, the desired end for which we have been justified, called, and predestined is:-

a. A distinctive feature; the highest pinnacle or distinction. A trait, which distinguishes something above the rest; it is splendor, honor, fullness of perfection, radiant beauty, and magnificence.

b. It is the pinnacle of God's majestic powers, His awesome beauty, His unsearchable knowledge, His indescribable wisdom, His holiness, His amazing strength, and His perfect love.

c. The developing state which follows salvation. As it is written; "To those who by persistence in doing good seek glory, honor and immortality, he will give eternal life."And, "Therefore I endure everything for the sake of the elect, that they too may obtain the salvation that is in Christ Jesus, with eternal glory" (Romans 2: 7, 10; 2 Timothy 2:10).)

d. A transformation by the Holy Spirit, dependent on the individual's assessment of the Lord's glory. For we all with unveiled face are beholding the glory of the Lord, and are being changed into his likeness from one degree of glory to another; for this comes from the Lord who is the Spirit" (2 Corinthians 3:18). The level of one's glory is dependent on the degree in which Christ is formed or magnified in the individual.

e. A developing state as a result of suffering [not wrongfully] but as a Christian. Considered to be greater than all present sufferings. "For I consider that the sufferings of this present time are not worth comparing with the glory that is to be revealed to us" (Romans 8:18).

f. The future state of all those who will appear with Jesus Christ at His return. Because, "When Christ who is our life appears, then we also will appear with him in glory" (Colossians 3:4).

God has called us to His eternal glory, as it is written, "To this He called you through our gospel, so that you may obtain the glory of our Lord Jesus Christ." And, "After we have suffered a little while, the God of all grace, who has called us to his eternal glory in Christ, will himself restore, establish, and strengthen us. To him be the dominion for ever and ever. Amen" (2 Thessalonians 2:14; 1 Peter 5:10).

Since we have been called to God's eternal glory, and we are being transformed from one degree of glory to another, depending on the image of the glory we have before us. What sort of image do we have before us, and how does the image of God's glory manifest itself?

The Prophet Ezekiel in describing the glory of God wrote; "Like the appearance of the bow that is in the cloud on the day of rain, so was the appearance of the brightness round about. Such was the appearance of the likeness of the glory of the Lord" (Ezekiel 1:28).

The rainbow is the sign of the covenant God made between Himself and man, and every living creature that is with man. In fact it is God's perpetual covenant with the earth, for thus says the Lord; "This is the sign of the covenant I am making between me and you and every living creature with you, a covenant for all generations to come: I have set my rainbow in the clouds, and it will be the sign of the covenant between me and the earth.

Whenever I bring clouds over the earth and the rainbow appears in the clouds, I will remember my covenant between me and you and all living creatures of every kind. Never again will the waters become a flood to destroy all life. Whenever the rainbow appears in the clouds, I will see it and remember the everlasting covenant between God and all living creatures of every kind on the earth."

So God said to Noah, 'This is the sign of the covenant I have established between me and all life on the earth" (Genesis 9:12-17).

The rainbow with its seven splendid colors depicts the seven attributes which when formulated together, produced the divine nature of God which is love.

The seven colors of the rainbow which depicts the glory of God are:-

1. Red - depicting our precious life we give in service to God and planet earth. It is the service of brotherly kindness

2. Orange- depicting godliness, our moral and virtuous living, by abstaining from what is evil, and be obedient to the word.

3. Yellow - depicting the genuineness of our faith which is more precious than gold that perishes, even though refined by fire – may be proved genuine and may result in praise glory and honor when Jesus Christ is revealed.

4. Green – depicting perseverance/ patience, a by-product from the testing of faith. Because, "The testing of faith develops perseverance. Perseverance must finish its work so that you may be mature and complete, not lacking anything" (James 1:2-3).

5. Blue – depicting the color of a clear blue sky, reflecting godly divine knowledge.

6. Indigo – depicting self control, standing between knowledge and virtue.

7. Violet – depicting virtue, which is the application of godly knowledge, with sacrificial love.

Virtue is more than simple moral goodness. It is a source of inner strength/power, by which the moral goodness is executed. It is the power which exercises or executes faith.

These seven traits as depicted by the colors of the rainbow, forms the composition of love, and therefore we should make every effort to add to our faith goodness; and to goodness knowledge; and to knowledge; self control; and to self-control, perseverance; and to perseverance, godliness; and to godliness, brotherly kindness; and to brotherly kindness, love.

For, "If you possess these qualities in increasing measure, they will keep you from being ineffective and unproductive in your knowledge of our Lord Jesus Christ. But if anyone does not have them, he is short-sighted and blind, and has forgotten that he has been cleansed from his past sins." (2 Peter1:5-9).

Our spiritual growth can also be measured by our relationship with the world. For it is written; "You adulterous people, don't you know that friendship with the world becomes an enemy of God? Anyone who chooses to be a friend of the world makes himself an enemy of God. Or do you think scripture says without reason that the spirit he caused to live in us envies intensely?

But he gives us more grace, that is why the scripture says: "God opposes the proud but gives grace to the humble." Submit yourselves, then, to God. Resist the devil, and he will flee from you. Draw near to God and he will draw near to you" (James 4:4-7).

We are therefore admonished saying; "Do not love the world or the things in the world. If anyone loves the world, love for the Father is not in him. For all that is in the world, the lust of the flesh, and the lust of the eyes and the pride of life, is not of the Father but is of the world" (1John 2:15-17).

Spiritual growth can also be measured by one's zeal and desire to worship and fellowship with God and His son Jesus Christ, by fellow-shipping with one another at God's appointed times, known as holy convocation.

May the eyes of our spiritual understanding be enlightened.

Chapter Three

The Spiritual Warfare

Due to man's duality there is a spiritual battle which goes on daily between the flesh and spirit.

The battle ground for this battle is the mind, in order to gain possession of it. Now since the mind controls the body, the objective of this battle is to gain control of the mind, so that the individual will use the members of his body to fulfill the will of his chosen master.

Our master is the one to whom we yield ourselves servants to obey. As free moral agents we choose our master, we surrender ourselves to whomsoever we will to obey, and the master has sovereignty only over what his subjects have surrendered.

Humans are not independent beings: they are servants either to the flesh, or to the spirit.

All mankind was born with a natural, carnal mind which is hostile to God, not subject to the laws of God, and neither can it ever be. This natural mind is not spiritual. It does not receive the gifts of the Spirit of God, for they are foolishness to him, and he is unable to understand them, because they are spiritually discerned.

In order for the natural carnal mind to understand the things of the Spirit, it must be revealed by the Holy Spirit, for this reason, "No one can say Jesus is Lord, except by the Holy Spirit.

But the death and resurrection of Jesus Christ has now made it possible for whosoever will, to have a spiritual mind. As it is written, "If then you have been raised with Christ, seek the things that are above, where Christ is seated at the right hand of God.'

"Set your minds on things that are above, not on things that are on earth. For you have died, and your life is hid with Christ in God." Now in Christ Jesus, you who were once far off have been brought near by the blood of Christ.

We can learn a lot from the apostle Paul concerning the reality and severity of this battle. He said, "I speak to you in human terms because of the weakness of your flesh. For just as you presented your members as slaves of uncleanness, and of lawlessness leading to more lawlessness, so now present your members as slaves of righteousness for holiness" (Romans 6:19).

The apostle Paul experienced the same struggle in life, he said, "I find this law at work: When I want to do good, evil is right there with me. For in my inner being I delight in God's law; but I see another law at work in the members of my body, warring against the law of my mind and making me a prisoner of the law of sin at work within my members".

Then he lamented and said, "What a wretched man I am! Who will rescue me from this body of death? Then he breathed a sigh of relief and said, "Thank be to God through Jesus Christ our Lord! So then, I myself in my mind am a slave to God's law, but in the sinful nature a slave to the law of sin" (Romans 7:21-23).

Human beings are creatures of habit, we grow and develop to become the individual we are, in the area we have trained ourselves to become, whether knowingly or unknowingly.

For example we have been instructed saying, "Little children, let no one deceive you, he who practices righteousness is righteous, just as he is righteous"(1John 3:7).

We practice to become what we want to become. Practice makes perfect, not in the sense of being flawless, because if one practice doing the wrong thing, he/she will end up as a complete failure, but perfect in the sense of adaptation, of mastering the art.

The flesh has an insatiable desire which cannot be contained. It becomes addicted to whatever practice/s it engaged itself in. The inner drive of this sinful nature is so powerful that the Lord said, "Now nothing that they propose to do will be withheld from them"(Genesis.11:6).

Human beings are free moral agents, having the prerogative to choose their master. They are not an independent being operating on their own, they are either a slave of sin, or a slave of righteousness.

Quoting the Apostle Paul again he said, "Don't you know that when you offer yourselves to someone to obey him as slaves, you are slaves to the one whom you obey - whether you are slaves to sin, which leads to death, or to obedience, which leads to righteousness? But thank be to God that, though you used to be slaves to sin, you wholeheartedly obeyed the form of teaching to which you were entrusted. You have been set free from sin and have become slaves to righteousness.

Our free moral agency is the power we have as God to choose. It is the power to choose good over evil, the kingdom of light over the kingdom of darkness, the life in the spirit over the life in the flesh, the commandment of God [righteousness] over lawlessness or vice verse.

Neither God nor Satan will force anyone to do anything. God will inspire thoughts in our mind, and Satan will tempt us through the passions and desires of the flesh, but it is left to us to yield. Because of the nature and power of our free moral agency, we are essentially a part and parcel of the architect of our destiny.

Nature of the Spiritual Warfare

Our spiritual battle is not only internal between the flesh and the spirit, but it is external as well.

We are engaged in an external battle for which we are forewarned saying, "Our struggle is not against flesh and blood, but against the rulers, against the authorities, against the powers of this dark world and against the spiritual forces of evil in the heavenly realms" (Ephesians 6:12).

To prepare ourselves for this battle we are reminded saying, "For though we live in the world, we do not wage war as the world does. The weapons we fight with are not the weapons of the world. On the contrary, they have divine power to demolish strongholds."

Now because of the reality and practicality of the warfare, it is imperative that we know the nature, or the premise on which the spiritual war is being fought.

The cause of this spiritual warfare is Satan's attempt to thwart God's master plan for the human race, thus making us the target.

When God created man, He created him in his image and likeness, and for man to have dominion over the fish of the sea, and the birds of the air, over the livestock, over the earth, and over all the creatures that moves along the ground. So God created man in his own image, in the image of God he created him; male and female he created them.

Unfortunately, with the exception of Jesus Christ, no other man has fulfilled God's plan. He alone exercised his dominion and authority over the earth.

Here are a few examples of how Jesus Christ demonstrated his power and authority over the earth.

On one occasion he was in a boat sleeping, and without

warning, a furious storm came upon the lake, so that the waves swept over the boat; so the disciples went and woke him up saying, "Lord save us! We are going to drown!"

Jesus' reply to them was, "You of little faith, why are you so afraid? Then he got up and rebuked the winds and the waves, and it was completely calm. The men were amazed and asked, "What kind of man is this? Even the wind and the waves obey him!" (Matthew 8:23-27)

Early one morning, Jesus was hungry. Seeing a fig tree by the road, he went up to it but found nothing on it except leaves. Then he said to it, "May you never bear fruit again!" Immediately the tree withered (Matthew 21:18-19).

On another occasion, Jesus was confronted with the question of paying temple taxes. Although as the Son of God, he was not required to pay taxes, nevertheless to avoid offending them he asked his disciples to, " Go to the sea and cast a hook, and take the first fish you catch; open its mouth and you will find a shekel. Take it and give it to them for my tax and yours" (Matthew 17:27).

There was also the incident where the disciples saw Jesus Christ actually walking on the sea, and Peter said to him, "Lord, if it is you, command me to come to you on the water." And in all accounts, Peter himself actually walked on the water to go to Jesus.

But when he saw that the wind was boisterous, he was afraid; and beginning to sink he cried out, saying, Lord, save me!"

And immediately Jesus stretched out his hand and caught him and said to him, "O you of little faith, why did you doubt" (Matthew 14:31)?

These examples are not merely miracles so to speak, but a

manifestation and demonstration of one exercising his authority, and dominion over the earth.

This is what it means to have dominion. To have dominion over the fish of the sea, one should be able to go where the fish go. To have dominion over the birds of the air, and should be able to travel where they travel.

Some of us may want to simply close our minds on these things, with the notion that this is beyond our reach. Fair enough, but let us not forget that, man was created to have dominion over the earth.

To verify the fact that this is what we were destined to become, after the episode with the fig tree, Jesus said to his disciples, "I tell you the truth, if you have faith and do not doubt, not only can you do what was done to the fig tree, but also you can say to this mountain, Go, throw yourself into the sea, and it will be done. If you believe, you will receive whatever you ask for in prayer" (Matthew 21:21-22).

When Peter began sinking whilst walking on the water, Jesus simply stretched out his hand and caught him and said, "You of little faith, why did you doubt?"

Unfortunately for us, it is quite difficult for us to attain this level of faith, by which we can take control, because, how are we to believe in him of whom we have never heard? And how are we to hear without a preacher? And how can men preach unless they are sent? You see faith comes from what is heard, and what is heard comes by the preaching of Christ.

To have dominion is to have commanding position over whatever you have dominion over. This is man's destiny to have dominion over the earth, even Satan and his demons that are now cast down to the earth. Satan knows this, and this is why he is so furious, and he is all out to destroy man.

Satan took away the initiative from Adam by deceiving Eve,

and caused them to disbelieved and disobeyed God.

He attempted to Kill Jesus Christ, as soon as he was born.

He tried to take the initiative away from Jesus Christ before he began his ministry, shortly after his forty days and forty nights fasting in the wilderness.

Remember one becomes the slave or servant to whom he/she yields to obey. This also applies to Satan and his demons.

If Jesus Christ had yielded to any of his requests, he would have relinquished his power and authority to him. It took Adam only one act of servitude to loose control over a whole empire.

Hence the reason why we are admonished to, "Resist the devil and he will flee from you" (James 4:7).

Satan succeeded in having Jesus killed on the cross, and thought that he had the victory. But little did he know that, the death of Jesus Christ, was, "God's secret wisdom, a wisdom that has been hidden and that God destined for our glory before time began.

None of the rulers of this age understood it, for if they had, they would not have crucified the Lord of glory" (1Corinthians 2:7-8).

Men and angels were created and ordained to fulfill different roles, and carry out different responsibilities.

Angels were created to worship God, and to minister to those who will inherit salvation. For to which of the angels did God ever say, "You are My Son; today I have begotten you. Or again, "I will be his Father, and he will be My Son"?

Again, to which of the angels did God ever say, "Sit at My right hand, until I make your enemies a footstool for your feet" (Hebrews 1:5, 13).

But to Jesus He said: "Your throne, O God, will last for ever and ever, and righteousness will be the scepter of your kingdom. You have loved righteousness and hated wickedness; therefore God, your God, has set you above your companions by anointing you with the oil of joy" (Hebrews 1:8-9).

Our consolation is that "We see Jesus, who was made a little lower than the angels, now crowned with glory and honor because he suffered death, so that by the grace of God he might taste death for everyone.

And in bringing many sons to glory, it was fitting that God, for whom and through whom everything exists, should make the author of their salvation perfect through suffering.

Therefore, both the one who makes men holy and those who are made holy are of the same family. So Jesus is not ashamed to call them brothers. He says, "I will declare your name to my brothers; in the presence of the congregation I will sing your praises."

And again, "I will put my trust in him."

And again he says, "Here am I and the children God has given me" (Hebrews 2:9-13).

This future hope for man is what triggers the jealousy, the envy, the hatred, the animosity in Satan against human beings.

Consider a being which the bible described as, "The model of perfection, full of wisdom and perfect in beauty. You were in Eden, the garden of God: every precious stone adorned you: ruby, topaz and emerald, chrysolite, onyx and jasper, sapphire, turquoise and beryl; your settings and mountings were made of gold; on the day you were created they were prepared.

You were anointed as a guardian cherub, for so I ordained you. You were on the holy mount of God; you walked among the fiery stones.

You were blameless in your ways from the day you were created till wickedness was found in you" (Ezekiel 28:12-15).

Consider what is going on in the mind of a being created with such splendor, now cast down to the earth, to be dominated by man who was formed from the dust of the ground!

What is even more outstanding is that, man was created in the image and likeness of God, signifying that, apart from being destined to have the same characteristics as God, they are destined to be one with God.

Because in praying for all believers Jesus said, "My prayer is not for them alone. I pray also for those who will believe in me through their message, that all of them may be one. Father, just as you in me and I am in you. May they also be in us, so that the world may believe that you have sent me: I have given them the glory that you gave me, that they may be one as we are one. I, in them; and you in me" (John 17:20-23).

Believers are God's workmanship, signifying that they are the materials, and the finished product which God is creating. They are regarded as God's field, God's building, and fellow workers with him.

The work that is being done is in Christ, whose body is God's spiritual temple, and believers are part of that body.

God's plan began with Jesus Christ in the Father, mankind in Jesus Christ, Jesus Christ in the believer, and God the Father in Jesus Christ. This completes the construction of God's spiritual temple, and God's purpose for man. Therefore, let us not loose heart in going through this spiritual battle. Although outwardly we are wasting away, yet inwardly we are being renewed day by day. For, our light and momentary troubles are achieving for us an eternal glory that far outweighs them all. So we fix our eyes not on what is seen, but on what is unseen. For what is seen is temporary, but what is unseen is eternal.

May the God of our Lord Jesus Christ, the Father of glory, give us a spirit of wisdom and of revelation in the knowledge of him, having the eyes of our hearts enlightened, that we may know what is the hope to which he has called us, what are the riches of his glorious inheritance in the saints, and what is the immeasurable greatness of his power in us who believe, according to the working of his great might which he accomplished in Christ when he raised him from the dead and made him sit at his right hand in the heavenly places, far above all rule and authority and power and dominion, and above every name that is named, not only in this age but also in that which is to come.

The Role of Angels

Jesus Christ made a remarkable statement saying, "Whoever confesses me before men, him the Son of Man also will confess before the angels of God, but he who denies me before men will be denied before the angels of God" (Luke 12:8-9).

Why should Jesus Christ the Son of God who by him all things were created; things in heaven and on earth, visible and invisible, whether thrones or powers or rulers or authorities, confess or deny one before the angels?

The answer is very simple; Angels are assigned to play a pivotal role in the affairs of human beings.

Angels are supernatural beings created by God before the foundation of the world and mankind. Surprisingly, they are not perfect beings, they are also vulnerable. History shows that one third of them followed Lucifer in his rebellion. It is stated that, "God did not spare the angels who sinned, but cast them into chain of darkness to be reserved for judgment" (2 Pet. 2:2-4).

Eliphaz the Temanite, one of Job's friends said to him, "Can a mortal be more righteous than God? Can a man be more pure than his maker? If he puts no trust in his servants and charges his angels with error; how much more those who dwell in houses of clay, whose foundation is in the dust who are crushed before a moth?" (Job. 4:17-21).

Angels are holy, wise, meek, obedient, powerful and invisible spiritual beings, they are loyal and faithful ministers of God, they excel in strength by heeding to the voice of God and fulfilling his word.

They like all other created beings praise the Lord. As it is written; "Praise the Lord! Praise the Lord from the heavens, praise him in the heights! Praise him, all his angels, praise him all his hosts! Praise him sun and moon praise him, all you shining stars! Praise him, you highest heavens, and you waters above the heavens! Let them praise the name of the Lord! For, he commanded, and they were created. And he established them for ever and ever; he fixed their bounds which cannot be passed" (Psalms 184:1-6).

Angels possess feelings and emotions because when God created the world it is said that they all sang together and shouted for joy. It is said that there is joy in the presence of the angels of God over one sinner who repents.

They are God's Ministers sent forth to minister for those who will inherit salvation.

The role they play in human affairs is to Guide, protect, deliver, comfort, provide for, and minister to and for the believers. It is stated that, "The angel of the Lord encamps all around those who fear him, and saved him out of all his troubles" (Psalms 34:7).

God gives his angels charge over his people. They are assigned to those who will inherit salvation.

Satan is fully aware of this hence the reason why when he brought Jesus to Jerusalem, and set him on the pinnacle of the temple, he said to him, "If you are the Son of God, throw yourself down from here. For it is written: 'He shall give his angels charge over you to keep you; and in their hands they shall bear you up, lest you dash your foot against a stone." This is a direct quotation from Psalms 91:11-12.

Angels however are not to be worshiped, they are created beings. We are to worship and serve only the Creator who is blessed for ever.

We are admonished saying, "Let no one defraud you of your reward, taking delight in false humility and worship of angels, intruding into those things which he has not seen, vainly puffed up by his fleshly mind" (Colossians 2:18).

It is important that we acknowledge the presence of the Holy angels who encamps around us. The world we live in is called this present evil world, and it is in subjection to angels.

Our daily struggles are not against flesh and blood, but are against spiritual hosts of wickedness in the heavenly places.

Our battles are spiritual in nature, and therefore we need spiritual help and intervention to protect and deliver us from our enemies. Because, "Even though we walk in the flesh, we do dot war according to the flesh. For the weapons of our warfare are not carnal but mighty in God for the pulling down of strong holds" (2 Corinthians 10:3-4).

Yes, Jesus confesses, or denies one before the angels because he delegates to them their specific duties. On behalf of the believer, they guide, provide, protect, deliver, direct activities, comfort, minister to, and eventually will gather the elect from one end of heaven to the other.

Whereas on behalf of the unbeliever, they are assigned to curse, cause destruction; bring about sudden death, pestilence and persecution.

Angels are loyal obedient servants of God and conduct their affairs diligently. Hence the reason we have been admonished saying, "When you vow a vow to God, do not delay paying it; for he has no pleasure in fools.

Pay what you vow. It is better that you should not vow than that you should vow and not pay. Let not your mouth lead you into sin, and do not say before the angel [messenger] that it was a mistake; why should God be angry at you voice, and destroy the work of your hands?

We are therefore encouraged to, "Let brotherly love

continue;' and, 'Do not neglect to show hospitality to strangers, for thereby some have entertained angels unawares" (Hebrews 13:1-2).

We need to be aware of the world in which we live, and the role which angels play in the lives of man. This present evil world is in subjection to angels. In reality, we are not contending against flesh and blood, but against the principalities, against the powers, against the world rulers of this present darkness, against the spiritual hosts of wickedness in the heavenly places, and for this reason, angels plays a very important role in the affairs of man and we should all be conscious of that.

Chapter Four

The Power of Choice

We all have the choice to choose the way of life above the other, which is the lesser of two evils. This is our greatest source of power, the choice of life or death, blessings or curses.

The choice of life or death; blessings or curses were established from the beginning of man's creation. It was represented by two (2) symbolic trees that were planted in the Garden of Eden. According to the scriptures; "The Lord God made all kinds of trees grow out of the ground—trees that were pleasing to the eye and good for food. In the middle of the garden were the tree of life and the tree of the knowledge of good and evil" (Genesis 2: 9).

God gave Adam specific instructions regarding the tree of the knowledge of good and evil when he said to him; "Of every tree of the garden you may freely eat; but of the tree of the knowledge of good and evil you shall not eat, for in the day that you eat of it you shall surely die"(Genesis 2:16-17).

But Satan who is man's adversary came along and said, "You will not surely die; for God knows that when you eat of it your eyes will be opened, and you will be like God, knowing good and evil."

So, "When the woman (Eve) saw that the fruit of the tree was good for food and pleasing to the eye, and also desirable for gaining wisdom, she took some and ate it. She also gave some to her husband, who was with her, and he ate it" (Genesis 3:4- 6)

The choice which they made afforded them power to choose for themselves what is right and what is wrong, but not without terrible consequences. The choice they made resulted in:-

A. Man becoming like God, having the power to know good and evil, and live independently from God, contrary to Him.

This is the power called sin, and which resides in the flesh. This way of life seems right to a man, but its end is the way of death.

B. Inevitable death of humanity. Although man was made mortal from the dust of the earth, He did not have to die, if he had made the right choice and partook of the other tree which was in the midst of the garden, he would have lived for ever.

C. Separation from God: Seeing that they had lost their heavenly dwelling (clothing) and was naked, they hid themselves from God. There is an earthly clothing, and a heavenly clothing.

D. Curses to the human race, and the whole ecological system. It is for this reason a woman ought not to usurp authority over a man, because Adam was not the one deceived; it was the woman who was deceived and sinned.

The other choice was to partake of the tree of life, and lived for ever. This tree represented Jesus Christ who is the way the truth and the life. After Adam and Eve made their choice to partake of the tree of the knowledge of good and evil, they were barred from the tree of life lest they would eat it and live for ever in their sinful nature.

Man will once again have access to the tree of life in the millennium.

From the fall of Adam, man was cut off from God, and He dealt with specific individuals like Noah, Job, Abraham, Isaac, and Jacob. He chose Abraham and entered into an everlasting covenant with Israel and his descendants. God had no dealings with man on a national or global scale.

In past generations He let all nations go their own way, hence the reason why there were no instituted laws, no Sabbath keeping, and no festival observance.

But when God chose the children of Israel to be a people for Himself, and a treasure above all the peoples on the face of the earth, He again gave them an opportunity to choose this time, between obedience and disobedience of His laws.

Moses, whom God raised to deliver the children of Israel from Egyptian bondage, and who led them to the Promise land said to them; "This commandment which I command you today, it is not too mysterious for you, nor is it too far off. It is not in heaven, that you should say, who will ascend into heaven for us and bring it to us, that we may hear it and do it?'

"Nor is it beyond the sea, that you should say, Who will go over the sea for us and bring it to us, that we may hear it and do it? But the word is very near you, in your mouth and in your heart, that you may do it. See I have set before you today life and good, death and evil" (Deuteronomy 30: 11-20: Deuteronomy. 11: 26-28).

God's dealing with the children of Israel was a substitute, or a copy of the reality.

For example;

Moses the deliverer was a type of Christ our Deliverer.

Egyptian Bondage was a type of our bondage in sin.

The Passover lamb was a type of Christ our Passover.

Israel's passage through the red sea was a type of our baptism or burial in the body of Christ at His death.

Israel being spiritually fed by eating of the Manna, and drinking from the Rock which followed them through their journey in the wilderness of sin (Zin), Was a type of communion, partaking of the bread and wine—the true bread from heaven, and the real drink which is given to sustain us through our journey in this world of sin, until we inherit the purchased possession to the praise of His glory.

The law which was given on the day of Pentecost was a type of the Holy Spirit whom the disciples received on the day of Pentecost.

The choice we have today is not the copy of the reality, but the reality itself. It is not a choice of obedience or disobedience to laws and regulations, but rather a choice of living. It is a choice of mindset, it is a choice between Jesus Christ and everything else.

Today, our righteousness is not of the law, but of faith and speaks this way, "Do not say in your heart, "Who will ascend into heaven? (That is to bring Christ down from above) or, "Who will descend into the abyss? (That is, to bring Christ up from the dead).

But what does it say? The word is near you even in your mouth and in your heart" (that is the word of faith which we preach); that if you confess with your mouth the Lord Jesus and believe in your heart that God has raised Him from the dead, you will be saved. For with the heart one believes to righteousness, and with the mouth confession is made to salvation" (Romans 10:5-11).

We must believe that Jesus Christ is the Lord God of the old Testament, and that everything points to him, and that he deserves our reverence and worship.

The Critical Choices of Life

The bible talks about a time of ignorance which God has overlooked: and now commands all men every where to repent.

This ignorance is the ignorance of the one and only true God who created the heavens and the earth, and man's duality, by which he is both the offspring of the first Adam which is natural and of a temporary existence; and the offspring of the Last Adam Jesus Christ, which is divine, spiritual and eternal.

For this reason man's life encompasses a series of choices which he has to make between these two diametrically opposite entities, which under no circumstances can or will co-exist together. These entities are at variance with each other, they are derived from two different sources, and any form of integration or merger between the two entities is unacceptable before God and is corruptible.

The choices one has to make because of his duality are:-:

1. The choice between adopting the devil as father: Or, God as our Father.

Jesus told the Jews who did not believe in him; "You are of your father the devil, and the desires of your father you want to do. He was a murderer from the beginning, not holding to the truth, for there is no truth in him. When he lies, he speaks his native language, for he is a liar and the father of lies" (John.8:44).

2. The choice of having the riches of this world [mammon] as our master: Or, God as our Master.

Jesus told his disciples, "No one can serve two masters. Either he will hate the one and love the other, or he will be devoted to the one and despise the other. You cannot serve

God and mammon" (Matthew 6:24).

3. The choice of having the leaders of this world as our king: Or, Jesus Christ as our King.

The Lord said to Samuel, "Heed the voice of the people in all that they say to you; for they have not rejected you, but they have rejected me that I should not reign over them" (1Samuel 8:7).

Samuel then said to the people, "You have today rejected your God, who Himself saved you out of all your adversities and your tribulations; and you have said to him, 'No, but set a king over us' (1Samuel 10:19)!

When the people realized the evil they had done in rejecting God who was their King, and asking for a king like the other nations, they said to Samuel, "Pray for your servants to the Lord your God, that we may not die; for we have added to all our sins the evil of asking a king for ourselves" (1Samuel 12:19).

Then Samuel said to the people, "Do not fear. You have done all this wickedness; yet do not turn aside from following the Lord, but serve the Lord with all your heart. And do not turn aside; for then you would go after empty things which cannot profit or deliver; for they are nothing.

For the Lord will not forsake his people, for his great name's sake. Because it has pleased the Lord to make you his people, moreover, as for me, far be it from me that I should sin against the Lord in ceasing to pray for you: but I will teach you the good and the right way. Only fear the Lord, and serve him in truth with all your heart; for consider what great things he has done for you. But if you still do wickedly, you shall be swept away, both you and your king" (1Samuel 12:20-25).

4. The choice of having our citizenship in the kingdom

of darkness, in this world: Or, having our citizenship in the Kingdom of light in heaven.

At conversion, God delivers us from the power of darkness, and translates us into the kingdom of the Son of his love, qualifying us to become partakers of the inheritance of the saints in the [kingdom of} light. (Colossians 1:12-13).

Unfortunately many live as enemies of the cross of Christ. Their destiny is destruction, their god is their stomach, and their glory is in their shame. Their mind is on earthy things.

But our citizenship is in heaven. And we eagerly await a Savior from there, the Lord Jesus Christ, who by the power that enables him to bring everything under his control, will transform our lowly bodies so that they will be like his glorious body"(Philippians 3:18-21).

5. The choice of living in accordance to the flesh: Or, living in accordance to the Spirit.

It is written; "So I say, live by the Spirit, and you will not gratify the desires of the sinful nature. For the sinful nature desires what is contrary to the Spirit and the Spirit what is contrary to the sinful nature. They are in conflict with each other, so that you do not do what you want" (Galatians 5:16-17).

6. The choice to live by the requirements of the law: Or, to live by faith in Jesus Christ.

Before faith came, we were kept under guard by the law, kept for the faith which would afterward be revealed. Therefore the law was our tutor to bring us to Christ, that we might be justified by faith. But after faith has come, we are no longer under a tutor" (Galatians 3:23-24).

Implying that, before one can come to have faith in Jesus Christ, and be justified by faith, he/she must first be tutored by the law, So as to be in conformity with Jesus Christ.

Because, faith comes by hearing: and hearing by the word of God.

7 The choice of having faith in the wisdom of men: Or, having faith in the power of God.

The apostle Paul said, "My speech and my preaching were not with persuasive words of human wisdom, but in demonstration of the Spirit and of power, that your faith should not be in the wisdom of men but in the power of God" (1Corinthians 2:4-5).

8. The choice of justification by works: Or justification by grace.

"If [justification is] by grace, then it is no longer of works; otherwise grace is no longer grace. But if it is of works, it is no longer grace; otherwise work is no longer work" (Romans 11:6).

9. The choice between two opinions, "If the Lord is God, follow him; but if Baal, then follow him" (1Kings18:21).

The choices we have to make is simply the choice between living the true, real, abundant life which Jesus Christ brought to humanity, instead of living the alternative way of life which man has chosen to live for himself which is a lesser of two evils.

These two diametrically opposite life styles are compared to two trees, each bearing its own fruit. You either make a tree good and its fruit good, or else make the tree bad and its fruit bad. Every good tree bears good fruit, but a bad tree bears bad fruit. A good tree cannot bear bad fruit, and a bad tree, cannot bear good fruit.

In like manner a good man brings good things out of the good stored up in him, and the evil man brings evil things out of the evil stored up in him. No spring can yield both salt water and fresh water from the same spring; nor can fresh water and bitter water issued from the same spring.

Our human body is the instrument that is used as either the servant of the flesh, or the servant of the spirit. Just as we have presented our members as slaves of uncleanness leading to more lawlessness, we must now present our members as slaves of righteousness for holiness. We are servants to whom we present ourselves slaves to obey, whether sin – the alternative way of man which seems right to him, and leads to death, or of obedience to the laws of God which leads to righteousness, and produces fruit to holiness, and the end everlasting.

Which will you choose?

Man's Greatest Challenge

Man's greatest challenge in life, is indeed the main objective for being alive, and this objective is to fulfill the will of God, which is the sanctification of the body, riding it from the filthy desires of the flesh, and becoming holy so that we can offer to him his offering, as a nation of priests.

In fact the reason for Christ's death and resurrection is to do away with the body of sin, for it is written; "For we know that our old self was crucified with him so that the body of sin might be done away with, that we should no longer be slaves to sin: because anyone who has died has been freed from sin" (Romans 6:6).

Sin is first and foremost the powerful insatiable lustful desire of the flesh which man yields to for self gratification, but it is also defined as:-

Transgressing God's laws.

All unrighteousness.

Omission of Duty.

Not acting from faith.

Thoughts of foolishness.

Sin manifest itself in what is termed, The works of the flesh; and human wisdom. For it is written, "Who is wise and understanding among you? Let him show it by his good life, by deeds done in humility that comes from wisdom. But if you harbor bitter envy and selfish ambition in your hearts, do not boast about it or deny the truth, Such wisdom does not come down from heavem but is earthly, unspiritual, of the devil. For where you have envy and selfish ambition, there you find disorder and every evil practice"(James 3:13-16).

Sin is the passion and lustful desires of the flesh that

competes with God. This is what we all give precedence before and above God and his laws. This is why things like sexual immorality, impurity, lust, evil desires and greed is termed idolatry, for we are placing our selfish, lustful desires before God.

A stern warning has been issued stating; "For of this you can be sure; no immoral, impure or greedy person, who is an idolater, has any inheritance in the kingdom of Christ and of God. Let no one deceive you with empty words, for because of such things God's wrath comes on those who are disobedient. Therefore do not be partners with them" (Ephesians 5:5; Colossians 3:5).

It is rather unfortunate that most people are ignorant of who they really are. They perceive themselves only as what David describes in Psalms 51:5, stating; "Surely I was sinful at birth, sinful from the time my mother conceived me." If this is the way one perceives him/herself to be, that is the way the person will live his/her live: for, "As a man thinks in his heart, so is he" (Proverbs 23:7).

What has eluded the minds of many people is the fact that Jesus Christ at His death and resurrection created a new generation of mankind in himself. He gave them a new life in the Spirit.

This new, inward, spiritually minded man was created in Christ Jesus in righteousness and true holiness at His resurrection..

Mankind therefore is both physical and spiritual. He has life which is spiritual and eternal in his spirit, and the breath of life which is physical and temporary in his flesh.

Before the advent of Jesus Christ, man had only the breath of life which they inherited from the first Adam As it is written;

"The first man Adam became a living being" He was of the

dust of the earth, and as was the earthly man, so are those who are of the earth. The spirit of man at that time was dead so to speak, because it was separated from God, because of the transgression of the first Adam.

Those who lived and died before the death and resurrection of Jesus Christ were offered life by Jesus Christ during the three days and three nights He spent in hell, preaching to the spirits in prison. For it is written; "I tell you the truth, a time is coming and has now come when the dead will hear the voice of the Son of God, and those who hear will live." .

"Christ died for sins once for all, He the righteous for the unrighteous, to bring them to God. He was put to death in the body but made alive by the Spirit, through whom also he went and preached to the spirits in prison who disobeyed long ago when God waited patiently in the days of Noah while the ark was being built" (John 5:25; 1Peter 3:18-19; 1Peter 4: 6).

Since the resurrection of Jesus Christ: all Praise to God and the Father of our Lord Jesus Christ! Who, in His great mercy has given us new birth into a living hope through the resurrection of Jesus Christ from the dead: This living hope is that of attaining the immortality of the human body, an inheritance that can never perish, spoil or fade away!

We inherited from the last Adam, the spirit man from heaven life, with the hope of destroying sin in the human body, so that what is now corruptible might become incorruptible, and what is now mortal might become immortal.

Therefore, we are admonished by the Apostle Paul saying, "Do not be deceived; evil company corrupts good habits. Awake to righteousness and do not sin; for some do not have the knowledge of God. I speak this to your shame" (1Corinthians 15:33-34).

It is really a shame for most people not to have known the reason why Jesus Christ took on the sinful nature of man, lived a perfect sinless life in sinful flesh; paid the penalty of sin which is death for all mankind; resurrected from the dead and gave to all a new life in the spirit, and not knowing the reason why Christ suffered all these things; and what is expected of us.

How many times have we seen or heard people who yield to the lustful desires and passions of the flesh, and giving the flesh priority over the Word of God say; God understand! When the reason why Christ died and rose again, is for us to, "No longer live for ourselves, but for Him who died for us and rose again." It is for us to do away with the body of sin (2 Corinthians 5:15; Romans 6:6).

Conquering sin in the flesh is not an automatic transformation which takes place at conversion. It is a concerted effort on the part of the individual, with the help of God's Holy Spirit, to whom we can go boldly to obtain mercy and find grace to help in our time of need, and by the renewing of the mind in the knowledge of Jesus Christ who created us.

We are the ones who are to exert the effort, according to our knowledge of Jesus Christ, with the help of God, and the power of his Spirit who does not give aid to angels but does give aid to the seed of Abraham, so as to put to death whatever belongs to our earthly nature: sexual immorality, impurity, lust. Evil desires and greed, which is idolatry.

Jesus Christ came in the flesh to set us a perfect example that we should follow His steps, He committed no sin and no deceit was found in His mouth. He was tempted in all points as we are being tempted, yet He never sinned.

During the days of Jesus' life on earth, He offered up prayers and petitions with loud cries and tears to the one who could save Him from death, and was heard because of His reverent submission.

Although He was a Son, He learned obedience from what He suffered and, once made perfect, He became the source of eternal salvation for all who obey Him and was designated by God to be High Priest in the order of Melchizedek

"God sent His own Son in the likeness of sinful man to be a sin offering. And so He condemned sin in sinful man, in order that the righteous requirements of the law might be fully met in us, who do not live according to the sinful nature but according to the Spirit" (Romans 8:3-4).

And, "Inasmuch as Christ suffered in His body, we are to also arm ourselves with the same attitude, because he who has suffered in his flesh is done with sin, and as a result, he does not live the rest of his earthly life for evil human desires (sin), but rather for the will of God" (1Peter 4: 1-2).

The antidote to defeat sin, (the lustful desires and passions of the flesh) is to live in accordance to the Spirit and becoming slaves to righteousness. "For having been set free from sin and having become slave to righteousness, or slaves to God, the benefit we reap leads to holiness (free from sin), and the result is everlasting life" or immortality of the human body (Romans 6: 18, 22).

Aspire to Become a Faithful and Profitable Servant

Since the main objective for man's salvation is to serve the Lord in righteousness and true holiness all the days of his life, it is imperative that we all aspire to perform our God given task as faithful and profitable servants.

Undoubtedly we have all been gifted with differing gifts according to the grace that is given to us, and should utilize them accordingly. If our gift is to prophecy, let us prophesy in proportion to our faith; if it is ministry, let us use it in our ministering; he who teaches, let him teach the way of God in accordance to the truth; he who exhorts in exhortation; he who gives with liberality; he who leads, with diligence; he who shows mercy, with cheerfulness.

Regardless of our differing gifts, as servants sanctified to serve the Lord, there are four things we all have in common. This thought is derived from following a discussion Jesus Christ had with his disciples.

On one occasion Jesus witnessed his disciples arguing among themselves, so he asked them, "What was it you argued among yourselves on the road? But they kept silent, for on the road they argued among themselves as to who would be the greatest.

Jesus having sat down called the twelve and said to them. "If anyone desires to be first, he shall be last of all and servant of all." Then he took a little child and sat him in the midst of them, and when he had taken him in his arms he said to them, "Whosoever receives one of these little children in my name receives me; and whoever receives me, receive not me but he who sent me"

Interestingly John answered and said, "Teacher, we saw a man driving out demons in your name and we told him to stop, because he was not one of us." I wish we all would pay a little more attention and consider carefully the fascinating answer Jesus Christ gave to John. He said, "Do not stop him, for no one who does a miracle in my name can in the next moment say anything bad about me, for whoever is not against us is for us" (Mark 9:38-40).

It is clearly stated in scriptures that, "No one can say that Jesus is Lord except by the Holy Spirit."

Jesus then gave a stern warning of the dangers and consequences of causing anyone who believes in him to stumble, even the members of our own body which causes us to sin. He said; "It would be better for him to be thrown into the sea with a large millstone tied around his neck: and it is better for one to enter the kingdom of God maimed with one hand, one foot, one eye, than to be physically whole and be thrown into hell.

At the heel of this serious warning, Christ's admonition to his disciples which applies to everyone without exception is:-

1. *Everyone will be seasoned with fire.*

Every one's life is a replica or a product of his thought because as a man thinks in his heart so is he. This is why the right teaching is so important. We all live what we believe, and our faith which is more precious than gold is bound to be tested with fire. The reason why whatever we believe and live will be tested by fire (trials and persecutions) it is simply to prove its genuineness, and may result in praise, glory and honor when Jesus Christ is revealed.

It is important to note that we are all rooted on one foundation, for no one can lay any foundation other than the one already laid, which is Jesus Christ. And whether we are aware of it or not, every single minute of our lives we are involve in the construction of our spiritual house.

Some people are building their spiritual house out of endurable material such as gold, silver, or costly stones, while others are constructing with wood, hay or straw. The sure thing is that, "Every one's work will be shown for what it is, because the Day will declare it, because it will be revealed by fire; and the fire will test each one's work, of what sort it is.

'If anyone's work which he/she has built on the one and only foundation which is Jesus Christ endures, he will receive a reward," a reward of his spiritual house, which is the immortality of his human body. But, "If anyone's work is burned, he will suffer loss." The loss of his spiritual house, an immortal body; 'but he him-self will be saved, yet so as through fire" (1Corinthians 3:12-15).

Remember, we are sanctified to serve the Lord in the construction of his temple, which is our body and we all share the same responsibility to rid our selves of our old sinful nature, and develop the nature of the new man which was created in Christ Jesus in righteousness and true holiness.

According to Job, "Man who is born of woman is a few days and full of trouble. He comes forth like a flower and fades away; he flees like a shadow and does not continue" (Job 14:1).

The wise King Solomon described man's life in this way; "For what has man for all his labor, and for the striving of his heart with which he has toiled under the sun? For all his days are sorrowful and his work grievous; even in the night his heart takes no rest" (Ecclesiastes 2:22-23).

No one therefore can escape the season of fire which is to the praise, honor and glory of God. Therefore, we are admonished to; "Do all things without murmuring and disputing, that you become blameless and harmless, children of God without fault in the midst of a crooked and perverse generation, among whom you shine as lights in the world"(Philippians 2:14-15).

The ideal thing is choosing the durable material such as faith without which it is impossible to please God, and to make every effort to add to faith goodness, and to goodness, knowledge, and to knowledge, self control; and to self control, perseverance; and to perseverance, godliness; and to godliness, brotherly kindness; and to brotherly kindness, love.

It is stated that, "If you possess these qualities in increasing measure, they will keep you from being ineffective and unproductive in your knowledge of our Lord Jesus Christ. But if anyone does not have them, he is short-sighted and blind, and has forgotten that he has been cleansed from his past sins" (2 Peter1:8-9).

We have the promise that, "If we do these things, we will never fall, and we will receive a rich welcome into the eternal kingdom of our Lord and Savior Jesus Christ" (2 Peter 1:10-11).

Our development and growth is patterned after Jesus Christ. "It is God who gave some to be apostles, some to be prophets, some to be evangelists, and some to be pastors and teachers, to prepare God's people for works of service, so that the body of Christ may be built up until we all reach unity in the faith and in the knowledge of the Son of God and become mature, attaining to the whole measure of the fullness of Christ" (Ephesians 4:11-13).

2. *Have salt in ourselves for every sacrifice will be seasoned with salt.*

To all believers Jesus said; "You are the salt of the earth; but if the salt loses its flavor, how shall it be seasoned? It is then good for nothing but to be thrown out and trampled underfoot by men' (Matthew 5"13). Therefore, He who has ears to hear let him hear!

Salt is indicative of purity, good influence, something which gives flavor, and endurable as the covenant of salt. This signifies that whatever we are offering to the Lord must be pure. We are admonished saying; "I beseech you, brothers. In view of God's mercy, to offer your bodies as living sacrifices, holy and pleasing to God, which is your spiritual act of worship" And, "Whether we eat or drink, or whatever we do, do all to the glory of God" (Romans 12:1; 1Corinthians 10:31).

What we all have in common is that whatever we do, or offer in the name of the Lord should be done with sincerity of heart, and reverence for the Lord. We are admonished saying; "Whatever you do, work at it with all your heart, as working for the Lord, not for men. Since you know that you will receive an inheritance from the Lord as a reward. It is the Lord Christ you are serving. Anyone who does wrong will be repaid for his wrong, and there is no favoritism" (Colossians 3: 22-25).

We are to let our speech be always full of grace, seasoned with salt, so that one may know how to answer everyone.

3. *Be at peace with each other*

If we truly understand and believe the comprehensive work of Christ, there would not be all the bickering and fighting among believers. Because according to Titus, "But when the kindness and the love of God our Savior toward man appeared, not by works of righteousness which we have done, but according to his mercy he saved us, through the washing of regeneration and renewing of the Holy Spirit, whom he poured out on us abundantly through Jesus Christ our Savior, that having been justified by his grace we should become heirs according to the hope of eternal life" (Titus 3:4-7).

According to the scriptures, "All things are of God, who has reconciled us to himself through Jesus Christ and has given to us the ministry of reconciliation, that is, that God was in Christ reconciling the world to himself, not imputing their trespasses to them, and has committed to us the word of reconciliation" (2Corinthians 5:18-19).

We are consecrated to live at peace with each other, we are admonished to, "Bear with one another, and forgiving one another, if anyone has a complaint against another; even as Christ forgave you, so you also must do" (Colossians 3:13). We are to pursue peace with all men, and holiness, without which no one will see the Lord.

4. Accountability

We must all make it our aim to be well pleasing to the Lord, for "We must all appear before the judgment seat of Christ, that each one may receive the things done in the body, according to what has been done, whether good or bad" (2 Corinthians 5:10).

"The one who knew his master's will, and did not prepare him self or do according to his will, shall be beaten with many stripes. But he who did not know, yet committed things worthy of stripes, shall be beaten with few, for everyone to whom much is given, from him much will be required; and to whom much has been committed, of him they will ask the more"(Luke 12:47-48).

Our task is to simply persuade others, out of love to believe and practice the truth, and be always ready. Because the Son of man is coming at an hour we do not expect. But if the servant says in his heart, my master is delaying his coming, and begins to beat the men servants and maid servants, and to eat and drink and be drunk, the master of that servant will come on a day when he is not looking for him, and at an hour when he is not aware, and will cut him in two and appoint him his portion with the unbelievers.

So instead of spending his entire life with Jesus Christ in his kingdom, ruling and reigning with him, he will spend part of his time in the outer darkness, where there will be weeping and gnashing of teeth.

Let us therefore aspire to be faithful and profitable servants, for thus says the Lord. "Who then is that faithful and wise steward, whom his master will make ruler over his household, to give them their portion of food in due season? Blessed is that servant whom his master will find so doing when he comes. Truly, I say to you that he will make him ruler over all that he has" (Luke 12:42-44).

The whole objective of Salvation is not just to be saved, but to come to the knowledge of our Lord and Savior Jesus Christ, and pattern our lives after him who has come to set us an example that we should follow his steps. Our sojourn here is to construct our spiritual house, the temple of the living God. Are we all going to strive to be a faithful and profitable servant?

Chapter Five

What is our Hope

Is our hope compatible to that of scriptures, or do we have a false hope? What is the hope of our salvation is it to go to heaven, as most people are hoping for, or is it to bear the image of the heavenly? One should not hope to attain something which he/she has not made provisions for. For example, one should not hope to attain a gold or silver medal at the Olympic Games if, he/she is not part of the Olympic squad, and he/she is not training for the Olympics.

In like manner one cannot rejoice in hope of the glory of God, unless he/she glories in tribulations (sufferings) knowing that tribulation produces perseverance; and perseverance character, and character hope. Our hope therefore, should be the expectation of what we will be as a result of the character we developed through perseverance in sufferings, as we strive to put on the image of the heavenly Man.

The basis of our hope is, God's plan for our future glory, as it is written; "I consider that our present sufferings are not worth comparing with the glory that will be revealed in us. The creation waits in eager expectation for the sons of God to be revealed. For the creation was subjected to frustration (futility), not by its own choice, but by the will of the one who subjected it, in hope that the creation itself will be liberated from its bondage to decay and brought into the glorious freedom of the children of God" (Romans 8:18-21).

Man is a spirit being imprisoned in a corrupt mortal body in hope of being delivered from the bondage of corruption. Our present condition is not by choice, but it is according to the will of Him who created us, and, " Who has saved us and called us with a holy (heavenly) calling, not according to our works, but according to His own purpose and grace which was given to us before time began but has now been revealed by the appearing of our Savior Jesus Christ, who has abolished death and brought life and immortality to light through the gospel" (2 Timothy 1:9-10).

Our hope is not to get saved to go to heaven. For, "By grace we have been saved, through faith, and this is not from ourselves, it is the gift of God—not by works, so that no one can boast." But rather, we were saved to share in the image and glory of God. For it is written, "Beloved, now we are children of God; and it has not yet been revealed what we shall be, but we know that when He is revealed, we shall be like Him, for we shall see Him as He is. And everyone who has this hope in Him purifies himself, just as He is pure" (1 John 3:2-3).

God saved us and gave us life in the spirit with the hope of attaining immortality. For, "When the kindness and the love of God our Savior toward man appeared, not by works of righteousness which we have done, but according to His mercy He saved us, through the washing of regeneration and renewing of the Holy Spirit, whom He poured out on us abundantly, through Jesus Christ our Savior, that having been justified by His grace we should become heirs according to the hope of eternal life" (Titus 3: 4-7).

It is the gift of eternal life which has been freely given to us that gives us hope of becoming heirs of God and joint heirs with Christ. It is Christ who Himself is eternal life, living in us in the person of the Holy Spirit that is our hope of glory.

In praying for Himself, Jesus said, "Father, the hour has come. Glorify your Son, that your Son also may glorify you, as you have given Him authority over all flesh, that He should give eternal life to as many as you have given Him. And this is eternal life, that they may know you, the only true God, and Jesus Christ whom you have sent" (John 17:3).

Our hope is to be like Jesus Christ, and to see Him as He is which He will manifest in His own time. He is the blessed and only potentate [the only absolute, Sovereign, mighty One], who alone has immortality, dwelling in unapproachable light, whom no man has seen or can see, to whom be honor and everlasting power. Amen.

We were saved with the hope of attaining immortality, without which no one can inherit the kingdom of God. Our hope, our joy, our crown of rejoicing is seeing each other in the presence of our Lord Jesus Christ at His coming.

The Holy Spirit of promise is the guarantee of our inheritance until the redemption of the purchased possession, to the praise of His glory. This purchased possession which is waiting to be redeemed to the praise of God's glory is our mortal body which was purchased with his own blood.

The whole creation groans and labors with birth pangs together until now. And not only they, but we also who have the first-fruits of the Spirit, even we ourselves groan within ourselves, eagerly waiting for the adoption, that is, the redemption of our body, for we were saved in this hope.

We were saved with the hope of doing away with the body of sin, and be no longer slaves of sin, while we eagerly wait for the Savior, the Lord Jesus Christ, who will transform our lowly body that it may be conformed to His glorious body, according to the working by which He is able even to subdue all things to Himself..

Our light affliction in combating sin in the flesh, is only for a moment, and it is working for us a far more exceeding and eternal weight of glory, considering that, the sufferings of this present time are not worthy to be compared with the glory which shall be revealed in us.

The various trials and sufferings are necessary to test the genuineness of our faith, which is much more precious than gold that perishes, and although it is tested by fire, it may be found to praise, honor, and glory at the revelation of Jesus Christ.

For we shall all stand before the judgment seat of Christ, and shall receive the things done in the body, according to what each one has done, whether good or bad. He who has sown to the flesh, will of the flesh reap corruption, and will not inherit the kingdom of God, but he who has sown in the Spirit will of the Spirit reap everlasting life, or immortality, and will inherit the kingdom.

Our hope therefore is to have Christ living in us, and if Christ is in us the body is dead because of sin, but the spirit is life because of righteousness. And if the Spirit of God who raised Jesus from the dead is living in us, He who raised Christ from the dead will also give life to our mortal bodies through the Spirit who lives in us.

The Spirit is alive in us because of righteousness, and righteousness is obedience to the commandments of God, especially obedience to the act of righteousness (Holy communion) which reaps the benefit of holiness, and the result is everlasting life or immortality of the body.

Our hope is that we will persevere in developing the character of Jesus Christ by condemning sin in the flesh, so that, "Just as we have borne the image (likeness) of the earthly man, so shall we also bear the image of the man from heaven" (1Corinthians 15:49).

Our hope is to receive honor as kings and priests and to reign with Jesus Christ on the earth. For we are to God "A chosen people, a royal priesthood, a holy nation, a people belonging to God, that we may declare the praises of him who called us out of darkness into his marvellous light, who once were not a people, but now are the people of God; who once had not received mercy, but now have received mercy" (1Peter 2:9-10).

Our hope is to be fashioned more and more like Jesus Christ until he is formed in us. It is for this reason he gave some to be apostles, some to be prophets, some to be evangelists, and some to be pastors and teachers, to prepare God's people for works of service, so that the body of Christ may be built up until we all reach unity in the faith and in the knowledge of the Son of God and become mature, attaining to the whole measure of the fulness of Christ.

And everyone who has this hope in Jesus Christ purifies himself, just as he is pure.

Only One Foundation

God has established for us a foundation on which to build our spiritual house, but each one should be careful on how he/she builds on it, for no one can lay any foundation other than the one which is already laid which is Jesus Christ. Some however will use different materials to build on that one foundation.

"If any man builds on this foundation using gold, silver, precious stones, wood, hay or straw, his work will be shown for what it is, because the Day will bring it to light. It will be revealed with fire, and the fire will test the quality of each man's work. If what he has built survives, he will receive his reward. If it is burnt up, he will suffer loss; he himself will be saved, but only as one escaping through the flames" (1Corinthians 3:12-15).

This reward is the immortality of our human body, with each having its own degree of glory. "The same way all flesh are not the same', because , "Men have one kind of flesh, animals have another, birds another and fish another, there are also heavenly bodies, and there are earthly bodies; but the splendor of the earthly bodies is one kind, and the splendor of the heavenly bodies is another.'

"The sun has one kind of splendor, the moon another and the stars another; and the billion of stars differ from another in splendor. So will it be with the resurrection of the dead. The body that is sown is perishable, it is raised imperishable; it is sown in dishonor, it is raised in glory; it is sown in weakness, it is raised in power; it is sown a natural body, it is raised a spiritual body. If there is a natural body, there is also a spiritual body" (1Corinthians 15:39-44). And this is our task here on earth, to build our permanent dwelling, the spiritual temple of God.

Ignorance of the law is no excuse. Some people told Jesus about the Galileans whose blood Pilate had mingled with their sacrifices. And He answered them saying; "Do you think that these Galileans were worse sinners than all the other Galileans, because they suffered thus?

I tell you, No; but unless you repent you will all like wise perish. Or those eighteen upon whom the tower in Siloam fell and killed them, do you think that they were worse offenders than all the others who dwelt in Jerusalem? I tell you, No; but unless you repent you will all likewise perish" (Luke 13:1-5).

No one is excusable before God, and there is no partiality with God, nor does He take a bribe. What is required of one is required of all. For we all were made in the similitude of God, and for one universal purpose. Therefore, "When the Lord Jesus is revealed from heaven in blazing fire with His powerful angels, He will punish those who do not know God and who do not obey the gospel of our Lord Jesus" (2 Thesalonians 1:7-8).

There is no excuse for anyone not to know God and not obeying the gospel of the Lord Jesus. Those who do not know God, and do not obey the gospel of Christ "Will suffer the punishment of everlasting destruction, and be shut out from the presence of the Lord and from the majesty of His power" (2 Thesalonians 1: 9).

The truth of the matter is, there is one universal purpose for all human life on earth, and there is absolutely no excuse for not knowing what this purpose is.

There are three main reasons why no one is excusable before God.

Predestination

Humanity is predestined to be the very image and likeness of

God. From the beginning God said; "Let us make man in our image, after our likeness." Now God is immortal, and He alone has immortality; and therefore, man is predestined to become immortal. Unfortunately, immortality is not a free gift as eternal life, it has to be attained, and it is attainable through righteousness which leads to holiness, and the end everlasting life or immortality. Humanity was created in Christ Jesus in holiness unto holiness for everlasting life.

To attain immortality one must rid the body of sin, by walking worthy of the calling, confessing our sins, and partaking of Holy Communion. This is the reason for Christ's death and resurrection, the reason for our calling and salvation, and this is the will of the Father.

<u>"What may be known of God have been clearly seen, being understood from what has been made, so that men are without excuse"</u> (Romans 1: 20)

For example:

Only the fool [one who misuses true wisdom] says in his heart, there is no God. "They are corrupt, they do abominable deeds, claiming to be wise, they became fools, and exchanged the glory of the immortal God for images resembling mortal man or birds or animals or reptiles. Therefore; God gave them over in the sinful desires of their heart to sexual impurity for the degrading of their bodies with one another. Even their women exchanged natural relations for unnatural ones.

In the same way the men also abandoned natural relations with women and are inflamed with lust for one another. Men committing indecent acts with other men, and received in themselves the due penalty for their perversion" (Romans 1:24-27).

Regardless what terminology is used to justify this act, such as, "Sexual preference" it is unnatural and inexcusable.

From the beginning God created male and female, then He blessed them, and said to them, "Be fruitful and multiply; fill the earth and subdue it." It is impossible for two men, or two women to multiply and be fruitful. And the reason for the two becoming one is for companionship, and to raise godly offspring unto the Lord.

From the beginning God made mankind male and female, and for this reason a man shall leave his father and mother and be joined to his wife and the two shall become one flesh; so they are no longer two, but one flesh.

Any abnormality in sexual behavior or development did not originate from God it is a result of broken laws. "For although they knew God, they did not glorify him as God, nor were they thankful to him, but their thinking became futile and their foolish hearts were darkened.

Although they claimed to be wise, they became fools and exchanged the glory of the immortal God for images made to look like mortal men and birds and animals and reptiles. For this reason God gave them over in the sinful desires of their hearts to sexual impurity for the degrading of their bodies with one another.

They exchanged the truth of God for the lie, and worshiped and served created things rather than the Creator... who is forever praised. Amen. And because of this, God gave them over to shameful lusts, even their women exchanged natural relations for unnatrual ones, in the same way the men also abandoned natural relations with women and were inflamed with lust for one another. Men committed indecents acts with other men, and received in themselves the due penalty for their perversion.

Furthermore, since they did not think it worth while to retain the knowledge of God, he gave them over to a depraved mind, to do what ought not to be done" (Romans 1:21-28).

Man is inexcusable before God because of his Conscience.

Conscience is the sense of right and wrong. It is ideas and feelings within a person that tell him when he is doing right and warn him when he is doing wrong. It is the inner judge of moral issues.

Man is endowed with a remnant of God's Spirit, and the breath [spirit] of the Almighty gives him understanding. Therefore, no one is excusable, we all should heed to our spirit who receives knowledge from the almighty God.

It is written; "As many as have sinned without law [knowledge] will perish without law, and as many as have sinned in the law [knowledgeable] will be judged by the law.

For when Gentiles, who do not have the law, by nature do the things contained in the law, these although not having the law, are a law to themselves who show the work of the law written in their hearts, their conscience also bearing witness, and between themselves their thoughts accusing or else excusing them on that day when, according to my gospel, God judges the secrets of men by Christ Jesus" (Romans 2:12-16).

It is said that, "The servant who knew his master's will: but did not make ready or act according to his will, shall receive a severe beating. But he who did not know, and did what deserved a beating, shall receive a light beating" (Luke 12: 47-48).

There is therefore absolutely no excuse.

Chapter Six

Freed from Sin

The bible states categorically that, "Whoever abides in Him does not sin. Whoever sins has neither seen Him nor known Him" (1John 3:6). The question is, "How plausible is this statement?" And how feasible it is to accomplish? To the majority of people this statement might sound outrageous, blasphemous, and even self righteous.

But we are further told that "Whoever has been born of God does not sin, for His seed remains in him; and he cannot sin, because he has been born of God" (1John 3: 9).

The big question is, "Did Jesus Christ fulfilled the purpose for which He was manifested?

Why did Jesus Christ the beloved Son of God took on the sinful nature of Man?

Jesus Christ took on the nature of man so as to;

Destroy the devil, his work, and release those who through fear of death were, all their lifetime subject to the bondage of sin and death. He appeared so that, he might take away our sins.

We ought to know and be assured that, "Our old man was crucified with Him, that the body of sin might be done away with, and that we should no longer be salves of sin. For he who has died, has been freed from sin" (Romans 6:6).

And we all died with Him. For it is written; "The love of Christ constrains us, because we are convinced that One died for all, and therefore all died, and He died for all, that those who live should no longer live for themselves but for Him who died for them and rose again" (2 Corinthians 5:14-15).

The good news is; we have been freed from sin. Sin [the

powerful passion and lusts of the flesh] no longer has dominion over us. We were begotten by God in Christ Jesus at His resurrection in righteousness and true holiness, and those who are counted worthy to attain the glorious resurrection from the dead will be sons of God, being sons of the resurrection.

Jesus Christ is the resurrection and the life, in Him we all live and move and have our being, we are also the offspring of God. In Him there is no sin, and we all stem out from Him. He is the vine we are the branches, and if the root is holy, so also are the branches.

Our main objective therefore is to do away with the body of sin, the insatiable desires of the flesh, the work of Satan, by abiding in Christ, that is; in the holy and righteous state in which we were created in Him, by resisting and mortifying the deeds of the body.

How can we abide, live, and remain in Christ?

We can abide and live in Christ by:-

a. Keeping His commandments, which guarantees the Holy Spirit, because the Holy Spirit is given to those who obey Him, and, "By this we know that we abide in Him and He in us, because He has given us of His Spirit" And, "Those who obey his commandments live in him, and he in them. And this is how we know that he lives in us: We know it by the Spirit he gave us" (Acts 5:32; 1John 4:13; 1John 3:24).

b. Acknowledging or confessing that Jesus is the Son of God, for it is written; "If anyone acknowledges that Jesus is the Son of God, God lives in him and he in God." And that God has raised Him from the dead, to give us life so that , "We no longer live for ourselves, but for Him who died for us and live again"(1John 4:15).

c. **Abiding in love**. For, "He who abides in love abides in God and God in him" (1John 4:12, 16).

d. Living worthy of the calling so as to partake of His flesh and blood through the ordinance of communion. For Jesus said, "He who eats my flesh and drinks my blood abides in me, and I in him" (John 6: 56)

Sin is conquerable.

No matter how impossible and unattainable conquering sin might appear to some, the insatiable desires of the flesh for self praise and gratification it is conquerable. It is for this purpose the Son of God was manifested, that He might destroy the works of the devil.

God made Him who knew no sin to be sin for us, that we might become the righteousness of God in Him. God sent His own Son in the likeness of sinful man to be a sin offering; and so He condemned sin in sinful man, in order that the righteous requirements of the law might be fully met in us, who do not live according to the sinful nature but according to the Spirit. .

Jesus Christ was tempted in all points as we are being tempted, yet He did not sin, and has set us an example that we should follow His steps. He Himself bore our sins in His body on the tree, so that we might die to sins and live for righteousness. He who has suffered in the flesh has ceased from sin; and as a result, he does not live the rest of his earthly life for evil human desires (sin), but rather for the will of God.

Listen to these astounding words, they are mind-boggling. "No one who lives in Him keeps on sinning. No one who continues to sin has either seen Him or known Him." Also, "He who does what is sinful is of the devil, because the devil has been sinning from the beginning." (1John 3: 6, 8)

Sin, the insatiable desire for self gratification cannot be contained. It is realized when, "One is drawn away by his own desires and enticed. Then when desire has conceived, it gives birth to sin, and sin, when it is full grown, brings forth death" (James 1:15). Fighting and quarrelling issued because of the insatiable desires that battle within us for self gratification.

However, there is hope, and help is available for us to fulfill the will of God, which is, "**Our sanctification**". There is a simple guideline we can follow, and go to God for help, and be victorious. He does not give aid to angels, but He does give aid to the seed of Abraham. Therefore we can come boldly to the throne of grace that we may obtain mercy and find grace to help in time of need.

The guideline we should follow to help us conquer sin is:-

1. Use God's word

Jesus Christ referred to God's word three times during His encounter with the devil, by saying, "It is written." He said, "Man shall not live by bread alone, but by every word that proceeds out of the mouth of God." The Psalmist David said, "I have hidden your word in my heart that I might not sin against you" (Matthew 4:4, 7, 10; Lukek 4:4, 8, 12 Psalms 119:11).

2. Guard the tongue.

"The tongue is said to be a fire, a world of evil among the parts of the body. It corrupts the whole person, sets the whole course of his life on fire, and is itself set on the fire by hell. It is from the outflow of the heart the mouth speaks; and out of the heart comes all evil thoughts etc. For this reason we are told; "Let every man be swift to hear, slow to speak, slow to wrath; for the wrath of man does not produce the righteousness of God" (James 3: 6, 1:19-20).

3. Avoid evil companions.

Evil company corrupts good habits: a little leaven leavens the whole lump, and we are not to share in the sins of others, but keep ourselves pure, and come back to our senses as we ought to and stop sinning.

4. **Walk in the Spirit**.

By being spiritually minded, set our minds on things above, and not on the things on the earth. Only when we walk in the Spirit, [in the nature of the Spirit Man from heaven—the Last Adam—Jesus Christ] will we not fulfill the lusts of the flesh, for the flesh lusts against the spirit, and the spirit against the flesh.

5. **Exercise Love.**

Hatred stirs up strife, but love covers all sins, we must lay down our lives for others, as Christ did for us. For this is how we know what love is: Jesus Christ laid down his life for us, and we ought to lay down our lives for our brothers.

If anyone has material possessions and sees his brother in need but has no pity on him, how can the love of God be in him? Dear children, let us not love in words or tongue but with actions and in truth. This then is how we know that we belong to the truth, and how we set out hearts at rest in his presence" (1John 3:16-19).

6. **Confess to the Lord.**

"If we say that we have no sin, we deceive ourselves and the truth is not in us." And, "If we claim we have not sinned, we make Him out to be a liar and His word has no place in our lives." But, "If we confess our sins, He is faithful and just to forgive us our sins and to cleanse us from all unrighteousness" (1Jn. 1:8-9).

7. **Go to the Advocate.**

If anyone sins, we have an Advocate with the Father, Jesus

Christ the righteous. And He Himself is the propitiation for our sins, by the offering of His blood for the remission of sins

The truth is, We have been set free from sin and therefore sin should no longer have dominion over us; it should no longer be our master, because we are no longer under law but under grace, but because of weakness of the flesh we need to go to our Advocate to interceed on our behalf.

Therefore as High Priest, it is appointed for Jesus Christ to offer gifts and sacrifices. He does not have to offer any sacrifices on behalf of Himself. He does not need daily, as those high priests, to offer up sacrifices, first for His own sins and then for the sins of the people.

This He did once for all when He offered Himself" by becoming sin for us." "For God made Him who knew no sin to be sin for us, so that we might become the righteousness of God in Him." Jesus Christ as High Priest was fitting for us, because He is holy, harmless, undefiled, separate from sinners, and has become higher than the heavens" (Hebrews 7:26-27; 2 Corinthians 5:21).

Nevertheless, to present anyone to the Father, Jesus Christ as the High Priest must offer an offering in order to intercede on our behalf. The scripture states, "He is also able to save to the uttermost those who come to God through Him, since He ever lives to make intercession for them.'

For, "Every High Priest is selected from among men and is appointed to represent them in matters related to God, to offer gifts and sacrifices for sins." Now since, "Every high priest is appointed to offer both gifts and sacrifices, it was necessary for this one (Jesus Christ) also to have something to offer" (Hebrews 7:25; 2:17; 5:1; 8:3).

Offerings have to be offered because of sin

Since no one can say, I have no sin Nor, I have not sinned, intercession must be made on our behalf before coming to God.

Thankfully, "we have a great High Priest who has passed through the heavens, Jesus the Son of God; let us hold fast our confession. For we do not have a High Priest who cannot sympathize with our weaknesses, but was in all points tempted as we are, yet without sin" (Hebrews 4:14-15).

Since we have such a compassionate High Priest, "Let us come boldly to the throne of grace, going forth to Him, outside the camp, bearing His reproach, so that, we may obtain mercy and find grace to help in time of need" (Hebrews 4:16; 13:13).

The reproach that we bear in coming before him is the symbol of his sacrifice.

The fallacy in today's form of worship is two-folds:- Redeemed Saints who continually sin, but believing that they can approach God's presence and obtain mercy, and find grace to help in time of need without presenting to the High Priest His perfect offering for sin, which fulfills the will of the Father, and;

Having a fine way of setting aside the commands of God in order to observe the traditions of men.

Learn To Put Our Trust in God

We are admonished in the Psalms saying; "Trust in him at all times, you people; pour out your heart before him: God is refuge for us."

The majority of people especially those who say they believe in God, profess to have trust in God, but in reality their trust is in the flesh.

Trusting God I am afraid is more profound than many of us have realized. To trust God is to have a firm belief or confidence in his honesty, truthfulness, justice, and power.

When an individual on his/her own volition surrenders, or gives up his/her life to God, trusting God signifies that the individual has covenanted with God to give him full control and jurisdiction over his/her life.

Now since surrendering one's life to God is a covenant between the individual and God, it is the individual's responsibility to allow God to have full control over his/her life, and believe it or not it is incumbent upon God in whom the individual has placed his/her trust, as a matter of responsibility and obligation to exercise full control over the individual.

In this regard we have been comforted with these words, "He who dwells in the shelter of the Most High, and abides in the shadow of the almighty, will say to the Lord, 'My refuge and my fortress; my God, in whom I trust.'

And because of the confidence and rest, due to the trust one has in God, "He will deliver you from the snare of the Fowler and from the deadly pestilence; he will cover you with his pinions, and under his wings you will find refuge. His faithfulness is a shield and buckler. You will not fear the terror of the night, nor the arrow that flies by day, nor the pestilence that stalks in darkness, nor the destruction that wastes at noonday. A thousand may fall at your side, ten thousand at your right hand; but it will not come near you. You will only look with your eyes and see the recompense of the wicked" (Psalms 91:1-8).

These promises are conditional, they do not occur automatically even though one professes to believe in God, it is God's duly responsibility to those who has made the Lord their refuge, who has placed their trust in God.

The psalmist continues, "Because (conditional) you have made the Lord your refuge, the Most High your habitation, no evil shall befall you, no disaster will come near your tent. For, he will give his angels charge of you, to guard you in all your ways, they will bear you up, lest you dash your foot against a stone. You will tread on the lion and the cobra, the young lion and the serpent you will trample under foot."

Again, "Because he cleaves to me in love, I will deliver him; I will protect him, because he knows my name. When he calls to me, I will answer him; I will be with him in trouble, I will rescue him and honor him. With long life I will satisfy him, and show him my salvation" (Psalms 91:9-16).

We can therefore have full trust and confidence in God to keep his part of the covenant, because as he says, "God is not man that he should lied, or a son of man that he should repent. Has he said, and will he not do it? Or has he spoken, and will he not fulfill it?"

For thus says the Lord, "... I am the Lord, I do not change; therefore, you are not consumed, O sons of Jacob" (Malachi 3:6).

Now since God in whom we place our trust and confidence to be our refuge, shelter, protection, safety, security from danger and trouble, and who is trustworthy and just, and does not change, why then should believers who profess to have trust in God, murmur, and complaint when things are not going well, especially our way?

Since we have been admonished to, "Do all things without complaining or arguing, so that you may become blameless and pure, children of God without fault, in a crooked and depraved generation, in which you shine like stars in the universe"(Philippians 2:14-15).

The reason why we are not to complaint and argue it is because, "It is God who works in us both to will and to do for his good pleasure" (Philippians 2:13).

Furthermore, we have been instructed saying, "All things works together for good to those who love God, to those who are the called according to his purpose" (Romans 8:28).

The obvious reason why those of us who claimed to have surrendered our lives to God become at times disillusioned, discouraged, despondent, disenchanted, fearful, doubtful and pessimistic, it is because we do not truly trust God, it is that simple.

Those who have placed their trust in God's Name, his Word, and Jesus Christ, should not place their trust in:

• Weapons to defend themselves against their enemies. For it is written in the Psalms; "It is through God we will push back our enemies, it is through God's name we trample our foes, we do not trust in our weapon, our weapon does not bring us victory, but God gives us victory over our enemies, he put our enemies to shame."

• Wealth: whether it be hefty solid bank account, a good comprehensive insurance, a good solid pension plan, a reliable investment, or a secure job: because, those who trust in their wealth and boast of their great riches, can by any means redeem his brother, nor give to God a ransom for him.

The instructions given to us by the Lord is, "Take heed and beware of covetousness, for one's life does not consist in the abundance of the things he possesses."

In light of this, Jesus Christ gave a parable of the ground of a certain rich man which yielded plentifully. And he thought within himself saying, "What shall I do, since I have no room to store my crops?" So he said. I will do this: I will pull down my barns and build greater, and there I will store my crops and my goods.

And I will say to my soul, soul, you have many goods laid up for many years; take your ease; eat, drink, and be merry," But God said to him, 'You fool! This night your soul will be required of you, then whose will those things be which you have provided? So is he who lays up treasures for himself, and is not rich toward God" (Luke. 12:15-21).

Instead of being anxious and fearful when things seems gloomy, we are admonished to; "Consider the birds of the air who do not sow or reap, have no store room or barn yet God feeds them. And consider how the lilies grow, they do not labor or spin: yet, even Solomon in all his glory was dressed like one of these. And if God feed the birds which have neither storehouse or barn: and clothes the grass, which today is in the field and tomorrow is thrown into the oven, how much more will he feed and clothe us, who are of more value than birds and lilies."

Therefore, we are not to set our hearts on what we will eat, or drink; nor have any anxious mind. For all these things the Gentiles seek after, and our Father knows that we need these things. But seek first the kingdom of God and all these things shall be added to you" (Matthew 6:28-33).

Those who have placed their trust in God are to be anxious for nothing, but in everything by prayer and supplications with thanksgiving, should make their prayers known to God; and the peace of God, which surpasses all understanding, will guide their hearts and minds through Christ Jesus.

If one who has surrendered his/her life to God becomes despondent, discouraged, fearful, and anxious when the situation looks bleak, it simply means that his/her trust is not in God, but in the things which makes him/her feels secure.

• Leaders: Those who have placed their trust in the Lord are admonished; "Not to put their trust in princes, in mortal men, who can not save, because when their spirit departs they return to the ground, on that very day their plans come to nothing" (Psalms 146:3-4).

• Man. For it is written; "Cursed is the man who trusts in man, and makes flesh his strength, whose heart depart from the Lord" (Jeremiah 17:5). One can never know when a man will stop being faithful to God, and turn away from the way of God.

• Works. Any one who places his/her trust in works and their treasures strengthens himself in his wickedness. For thus says the Lord; "Let not the wise man glory in his wisdom, let not the mighty man glory in his might, nor let the rich man glory in his riches, but let him who glories glory in this, that he understands and knows me, that I am the Lord, exercising loving kindness, judgment and righteousness in the earth. For in these I delight," says the Lord" (Jeremiah 9:23; Jeremiah 48:7; Psalms 52:7).

• Righteousness: For thus says the Lord, "When I say to the righteous that he shall surely live, but he trusts in his own righteousness and commits iniquity, none of his righteous works shall be remembered; but because of the iniquity that he has committed he shall die" (Ezekiel 33:13).

One who has surrendered his/her life to God has his/her trust only in:

• God's Name. As it is written, "Our soul waits for the Lord; he is our help and our shield. For our heart shall rejoice in him, because we have trusted in his holy name" (Psalms 33:20-21).

• In God's Word. According to the Psalmist David, "Let your mercies come also to me, O Lord – your salvation according to your word, so shall I have an answer for him who reproaches me, for I trust in your word" (Psalms 119:41-42)

• In Christ; in whose name Gentiles will trust (Matthew 12:21).

Those of us who profess to have surrendered our lives to God: let us truly examine ourselves in this time of global financial crisis as to where our trust is, whether it is in God, or in our own security!

We have been admonished saying, "Trust in him at all times, you people; pour out your heart before him; God is a refuge for us." He is faithful in keeping his part of the covenant let us keep our part of the covenant by learning to trust him.

Have You Proved That The Lord Is Gracious?

Most people who have come to know the Lord will agree that the Lord is gracious. They can testify what the Lord has done for them. But boasting, pronouncing, or proclaiming that the Lord is gracious is no proof that one has indeed tasted the graciousness of the Lord.

Many are treating the graciousness of the Lord like the nine out of the ten lepers who were cleansed, but it was not found in them to return and give glory to God. Scriptures are replete with examples showing, that it requires more than simple expression of words to testify of the Lord's graciousness.

For example, quoting the prophet Isaiah Jesus said; "Well did Isaiah prophesy of you hypocrites, as it is written; "This people honors me with their lips, but their heart is far from me" (Mark 7:6).
Jesus is quoted saying, "But why do you call Me Lord, Lord, and do not do the things which I say?" (Luke 6:46)
It is prophesied that many (not the few) will come in the name of Christ, saying, that He (Jesus) is the Christ (saying how gracious He is), and shall deceive many.

Concerning entry into the kingdom of God, Jesus instructed His disciples saying, "Strive to enter through the narrow gate, for many, I say to you, will seek to enter and will not be able."

Why? Because, "when once the master of the house has risen up and shut the door, and you begin to stand outside and knock at the door; saying, Lord, Lord, open for us, and He will answer and say to you, I do not know you, where are you from," then you will begin to say, "We ate and drank in your presence (we lavished your graciousness), and you taught in our streets." But He will say, "I tell you I do not know you, where are you from. Depart from me, all you workers of iniquity"(Luke13:24-27).

Christ is quoted again saying, "Not everyone who says to Me, Lord, Lord, shall enter the kingdom of heaven, but he who does the will of My Father in heaven. Many will say to me in that day, Lord, Lord, have we not prophesied in your name, cast out demons in your name, and done many wonders in your name? And then I will declare to them, "I never knew you! Depart from me, you who practice lawlessness!" (Matthew 7:21-23).

One should underline the two words, **Iniquity** and **Lawlessness**, and find the true definition of these two words.

It takes more than just lips service to testify that the Lord is gracious. For, "He makes His sun rise on the evil and on the good, and sends rain on the just and on the unjust" (Matthew 5:45).

God's graciousness is simply a witness or testimony of Himself. In bygone generations God allowed all nations to walk in their own ways. Nevertheless He did not leave Himself without witness, in that He did good gave rain from heaven and fruitful seasons, filling man's hearts with food and gladness (Acts14:16-17.

Hence, both the good and the evil; the just and the unjust can say with their mouths that the Lord is gracious, because of His goodness.

But if indeed we have tasted that the Lord is gracious it will be manifested in us in eight (8) ways.

1. By having the fear of God.

The fear of God is to depart from evil, it is to hate evil, pride and arrogance and the evil way (Proverbs 3:7, 8:13).

The Psalmist David defined the fear of God by saying,

"Come you children, listen to me; I will teach you the fear of the Lord. Who is the man who desires life, and loves many days that he may seek good! Keep you tongue from evil, and your lips from speaking guile. Depart from evil, and do good; seek peace, and pursue it" (Psalms .34:11-14).

The Apostle Peter's understanding of the taste of God's graciousness is by, "Laying aside all malice, all guile, hypocrisy, envy, and all evil speaking" (1Peter 2:1).

The sad and unfortunate thing however, is that, the majority of people do not know what is evil! They equate evil to the works, or the produce of evil. We often hear comments such as, "I am not a bad person, I do not kill, I do not steal, I am just flirting around a bit," or, "I just like my parties."

The irony of truth is, there is no middle ground between good and evil. One is either good or evil. Jesus said, "Either make a tree good and its fruit good, or else make the tree bad and its fruit bad. For a tree is known by its fruit" (Matthew 12:33).

Sin, evil, iniquity, lawlessness is man's evil independent nature. It is the desire to walk after the imaginations of one's own heart, forsaking the way of the Lord, and doing what seems right in one's own eye. It is from within the independent evil nature of man proceed evil thoughts, adulteries, fornication, murders, thefts, covetousness, wickedness, deceit, licentiousness, an evil eye, blasphemy, pride foolishness etc (Mark 7:20-23).

According to the Prophet Jeremiah,"The heart is deceitful above all things and desperately wicked who can know it."

Therefore, who is a good and righteous man? And who is an evil and lawless man? A good and righteous man is one whose steps are ordered by the Lord, he walks in accordance to the laws of God. An evil and lawless man is one who disdain and disobeys the laws of God and directs his own steps.

There are only two ways of life, the one which is directed by the Lord, and brings blessings and life. The other is the one which is according to man's own imaginations, according to the flesh and results in curses and death. As it is written, "There is a way that seems right to a man, but its end is the way of death" (Proverbs 14:12, 16:25).

The only thing that stands between good and evil is "**Repentance**".

Jesus said, "I know your works, that you are neither cold nor hot. I could wish you were cold or hot, so then because you are lukewarm and neither cold nor hot; I will spew (spit, vomit) you out of my mouth" (Revelation 3:15).

Man is distinguished before God as either being good or evil; righteous or wicked, obedient or disobedient. The word of the Lord says, "The righteousness of the righteous man shall not deliver him in the day of his transgression; as for the wickedness of the wicked, he shall not fall because of it in the day that he turns from his wickedness; nor shall the righteous be able to live because of his righteousness in the day that he sins" (Ezekiel 18:20-32, 33:12-20).

God's admonition to all humanity is, "As I live, says the Lord God, I have no pleasure in the death of the wicked, but that the wicked turn from his way and live. Turn, turn from your evil ways! For why should you die: O house of Israel? (Ezekiel 33:11).

All sins with the exception of the unpardonable sin are equally guilty and forgivable before God. We are therefore admonished saying, "Wash yourselves make yourselves clean; put away the evil of your doings from before my eyes.

Cease to do evil, learn to do good; seek justice, reprove the oppressor; defend the fatherless, plead for the widow. Come now, and let us reason together, says the Lord, though your sins are like scarlet, they shall be as white as snow; though they are red like crimson, they shall be as wool" (Isaiah 1:16-18).

The unpardonable sin is blasphemy against the Holy Spirit. We are instructed saying, "If anyone sees his brother committing a sin, which does not lead to death, he will ask, and He (God) will give him life for those who commit sin not leading to death.

There is a sin leading to death. I do not say that he should pray about that. All unrighteousness (walking after man's own heart, and not according to God's law) is sin, and there is sin not leading to death" (1John 5:16-17).

Jesus said, " Assuredly, I say to you, all sins will be forgiven the sons of men, and whatever blasphemies they may utter, but he who blasphemes against the Holy Spirit never has forgiveness, but is subject to eternal condemnation" (Mark 3:29, Matthew 12:31-32. Luke.12:10).

Sin therefore is categorized in only two categories, (viz.)
Sin leading to death; and sin not leading to death.
Sin not leading to death is forgiven upon repentance. "If we confess our sins, He is faithful and just to forgive us our sins and to cleanse us from all unrighteousness" (1John 1:9).

When a sin, a violation, or straying away from the way of the Lord is confessed; the old way has to be forsaken; and not to be regretted (Proverbs 28:13).

For godly sorrow produces repentance to salvation, not to be regretted; but the sorrow of this world produces death. Hence, if we indeed have proven that the Lord is gracious, let us fear God, by departing from evil. That is, from directing our own steps, walking in accordance to the flesh: and let us follow the way ordained, and established by God.

If we have indeed proven that the Lord is gracious, it will stimulate the proper fear in us, which is, to stand in awe, in reverence, in high respect and esteem of His being, and give Him the honor and the glory which is due unto him.

There are Six (6) motivating factors which should stimulate the proper fear of the Lord.

* The first motivating factor is His Sovereignty or Majesty.

As stated in Jeremiah 5:22, "Do you not fear me? Says the Lord! Will you not tremble at my presence; who have placed the sand as a bound of the sea, by a perpetual decree that it cannot pass beyond it? And though its waves toss to and fro, yet they cannot prevail; though they roar, yet they cannot pass over it.'

"But this people has a defiant and rebellious heart; they have revolted and departed, they do not say in their heart, let us now fear the Lord our God, who gives rain, both the former and the latter in its season, He reserves for us the appointed weeks of the harvest. Your iniquities have turned these things away, and your sins have withheld good things from you."

Holding God in high esteem and honor is His rightful due. For, "Inasmuch as there is none like you, O Lord (you are great, and your name is great in might), who would not fear You, O King of the nations? For this is your rightful due, for among all the wise men of the nations, and in all their kingdoms, there is none like you? (Jeremiah 10:6-7).

To openly demonstrate one's fear of the one and only true God, who created the heavens, the earth, the seas, and springs of water, God has appointed specific days and times so that His people can come together to reverence His name, and give Him glory and honor.

For, "who in the heavens can be likened to the Lord? God is greatly to be praised in the assembly of the saints (which they are admonished not to forsake, even though not commanded), and to be held in reverence by all those who are around Him" (Psalms 89:6-7).

The appointed times which honor and glorify the Lord as the one and only true God, who created the heavens, the earth, the seas, and the springs of water are His Sabbaths. The Lord said, "You shall keep my Sabbaths and reverence my sanctuary: I am the Lord" (Leviticus 19:30, 26:2).

Again He said, "Surely my Sabbaths (plural) you shall keep for it is a sign between me and you through out your generations, that you may know that I am the Lord who sanctifies you" (Exodus 31:1`3).

Apart from the weekly Sabbath, the Lord has appointed three times or seasons in the year, when his people should appear before him as the Lord God. (Exodus 23:14-17, 34:18-24, Leviticus 23:1-4).

The Sabbaths are blessed, sanctified, and hallowed. It is a time of refreshing, rejoicing, and celebration. The word of the Lord says, "I am the Lord your God; walk in my statutes, keep my judgments, and do them; hallow my Sabbaths, and they will be a sign between me and you, that you may know that I am the Lord your God" (Ezekiel 20:19-20, 44:24, Isaiah 58:13-14, Jeremiah 17:22-27).

The true significance of the Sabbaths is to make us aware, or to remind us that The Lord is God.

What relevance has the Sabbath to a Gentile?

Gentiles who at one time "were without Christ, being aliens from the commonwealth of Israel, and strangers from the covenants of promise, having (at that time) no hope, and without God in the world, but now, in Christ Jesus, Gentiles who once were far off have been made near by the blood of Christ.

For He (Christ) Himself is our peace, who has made both (Jews and Gentiles) one, and has broken down the middle wall of division between us" giving Gentiles now the equal opportunity to rejoice and glorify God (not in isolation or in opposition, but rather) together with the children of Israel.

Therefore, we are told, "receive one another, just as Christ also received us, to the glory of God. Now I say that Jesus Christ has become a servant to the circumcision for the truth of God (to preserve and perpetuate God's truth), to confirm the promises made to the fathers, and that the Gentiles might glorify God for His mercy, as it is written:

"For this reason I will confess to you among the Gentiles, and sing to Your name". And again He says; "Rejoice, O Gentiles, with His people!"(Romans 15:7-10, Deuteronomy 32:43).

When someone appears before the Lord on days which He has not appointed and sanctified, it becomes an abomination. For thus says the Lord, "When you come to appear before me, who has required this from your hand to trample my courts?
Remember, the Lord has specifically ordained appointed times for His people to come before Him, to glorify and give reverence to His name as the one and only true God who created the heavens, the earth, and the streams of water. Only God has the prerogative to set aside a day and designate it as being a holy day, and to designate an assembly as being sacred and holy.

We are admonished in Revelation 14: 7 to, "Fear God and give glory to Him, for the hour of His judgment has come: and worship Him who made heaven and earth, the sea and springs of water." The only sign the Lord God gave to identify Himself as the Creator of heaven and earth is His

Weekly Sabbath. For thus the Lord says, "The children of Israel shall keep (observe, celebrate) the Sabbath, throughout their generation as a perpetual covenant. It (the Sabbath) is a sign between me and the children of Israel forever.'

Why? What is the rationale! "For in six days the Lord made the heavens and the earth, and on the seventh day He rested and was refreshed" (Exodus 31:16-17).

Therefore, those who appear before the Lord and trample His courts on days which He has not appointed, He says to them, "Bring no more futile sacrifices; incense is an abomination to Me. The new moons, the Sabbaths, and the calling of assemblies- I cannot endure iniquity and the sacred meeting. Your new moons and your (not mine) appointed feasts my soul hates.

"They are a trouble to me I am weary of bearing them. When you spread out your hands, I will hide my face from you; Even though you make many prayers, I will not hear. Your hands are full of blood" (Isaiah 1:12-13).

* The second motivating factor for the rightful fear of God is His Holiness.

Holiness is the unique quality of divinity; a life totally void and separated from sin. Therefore, we are instructed to be "as obedient children, not conforming ourselves to the former lusts, as in our ignorance, but as he who has called us is holy, we also be holy in all our conduct, because it is written, "Be holy, for I am holy" (1Peter 1:14-16); this should generate a tremendous measure of fear in us, if indeed we have proven that the Lord is gracious.

Holiness is purity, completely free from defilement and profanity. We are to give unto the Lord the glory due to His name; and worship the Lord in the beauty of holiness.

Holiness is associated to people, time or object, consecrated to God for holy use. Christians are called a chosen generation, a royal priesthood, a holy nation, God's own special people, that they may proclaim the praises of Him who called them out of darkness into His marvelous light.

This again should stimulate the rightful fear in every one who has indeed proven that the Lord is gracious. To the chosen people of God, He says; " I am the Lord who brings you up out of the land of Egypt (sin), to be your God, you shall therefore be holy, for I am holy" (Leviticus 11:45). Not only has God set apart His people for holy use, He has also set apart certain things as holy, and for holy use.

The word of the Lord came to Ezekiel saying, "Her priests (Israel's) have violated My law and profaned My holy things; they have not distinguished (make a distinction) between the holy and the unholy (profane), nor have they made known the difference between the unclean and the clean; and they have hidden their eyes from my Sabbaths, so that I am profaned among them" (Ezekiel 22:26).

Therefore, having a blind eye to the Sabbaths, especially when Jesus Christ said, emphatically, "The Sabbath was made for man, and not man for the Sabbath, Therefore the Son of Man is also Lord of the Sabbath" is a dishonor to God (Mark 2:27-28).

For Christ to be Lord (Master) of something holy as the Sabbath, should generate a certain amount of fear in those who have indeed proven that the Lord is gracious. Closing one's eye to the holiness of the Sabbaths is profanity.

Having the rightful fear of God, because of His holiness, should stimulate the awareness of making a clear distinction between holy and unholy, and between unclean and clean (Leviticus 10:10).

One of the Holy things of God is His law. We are told that, "the law is holy, and the commandment holy and just and good" (Romans 7:12), and within the context of the holy commandment, we are specifically reminded saying; "Remember the Sabbath day to keep it holy." Because, "the Lord blessed the Sabbath day and hallowed it (made it holy)" (Exodus 20:8, 11).

There are also specific times of holy convocations or holy assemblies, which the Lord specifically instituted. The Lord spoke to Moses saying, "Speak to the children of Israel, and say to them; the feasts of the Lord, which you shall proclaim to be holy convocations, these are my feasts". Again He said, "These are the feasts of the Lord, holy convocations which you shall proclaim at their appointed times" (Leviticus 23:2-4, 7, 8, 21, 24, 32, 35, 36, 37).

God alone is holy, and He alone can sanctify anything and proclaim it holy. He has set apart holy times to worship Him in the beauty of holiness. Each appointed feast or holy convocation commemorates an event which the Lord has made in His master plan for the salvation of humanity, and they also foreshadows things to come.

* The third motivating factor which ought to stimulate the rightful fear of God in those who have indeed proven that He is gracious is His Forgiveness;

It is written, "If you, Lord, should mark iniquities, O Lord, who could stand? But there is forgiveness with you, that you may be feared (Psalms 130:3-4).

Thankfully, "the Lord has not dealt with us according to our sins, nor punished us according to our iniquities; but he is merciful and gracious, slow to anger, and abounding in mercy. He will not always strive with us, nor will He keep His anger for ever"(Psalms 103:8-10).

The willingness for the Lord to forgive ought to stimulate the rightful fear in us, by holding Him in high esteem, reverence, adoration, and departing from evil. For, "If we say that we have no sin, we deceive ourselves, and the truth is not in us. If we confess our sins, He is faithful and just to forgive us our sins, and to cleanse us from all unrighteousness. If we say we have not sinned, we make Him a liar, and His word is not in us" (1John 1:8-10).

The gracious thing is that, Jesus Christ has made all the provisions for his people to live in holiness, and be constantly cleansed of their sins, through the cup of the New Covenant (agreement) which he instituted on the night before his death. For it is written; "For the life of a creature is in the blood, and I have given it to you to make atonement for yourselves on the altar; it is the blood that makes atonement for one's life" (Leviticus 17:11).

The cardinal error which most people make is, accepting sin as part of their new nature. We often hear comments such as, "God understands!" when someone exercises a lack of faith by not trusting God, or being disobedient, or exercising a lack of self control, by habitually living in sin.

This is so prevalent, because the basic assumption is, God understands their needs, their predicament, the weakness of the flesh, and therefore will sympathize with them when they compromise with sin.

But what does the Lord truly understands? What the Lord understands is this "My little children, these things I write to you that you may not sin" (signifying that there is the possibility of not sinning). And if anyone sins (not and when anyone sins, as though it is expected, but "IF" signifying that it is optional), we have an Advocate with the Father, Jesus Christ the righteous" (1John 2:1).

What the Lord understands and sympathizes with us is, "As

a father pities his children, so the Lord pities those who fear Him. For He knows our frame; He remembers that we are dust" (Psalms 103:13-14).

Notice; His pity is not towards those exercising lack of faith, or lack of self control or who violate His laws with impunity, but towards those who fear Him. That is, those who departs from evil. We are told that, "The mercy of the Lord is from everlasting to everlasting on those who fear Him, and His righteousness to our children children, to such as keep His covenant, and to those who remember His commandments to do them" (Psalms 103:17-18).

The Lord pities those who strive for excellence, for thus says the Lord; "You shall be perfect, just as your Father in heaven is perfect". Those who strive to enter the narrow way; those who, when faced with trials and temptations while pursuing the right path, will boldly come to the throne of grace, so that they may obtain mercy and find grace to help in time of need. For, "Indeed, He does not give aid to angels, but He does give aid to the seed of Abraham" (Hebrews 4: 16, 2: 16).

Furthermore, we do not have a High Priest who cannot sympathize with our weaknesses, but was in all points tempted as we are, yet without sin.

And, "To this we were called, because Christ also suffered for us (in the flesh), leaving us an example, that we should follow His steps: Who committed no sin, nor was guile found in His mouth" (1Peter 2: 22).

Therefore, since Christ suffered for us in the flesh, we are to arm ourselves with the same mind, for he who has suffered in the flesh has ceased from sin" (1Peter 4:1).

Yes, if indeed we have proved that the Lord is gracious, his forgiving mercy will stimulate the right fear of God in us, and we will strive to give unto Him the honor, the reverence, and the glory which is due to his name. We will depart from evil. That is, not allowing our independent human nature, which entices man to walk after the imagination of their own evil heart, and which is deceitful above all things and desperately wicked to control us, but we would be walking according to the righteous law, the way of God.

* The fourth motivating factor which ought to stimulate the rightful fear of the Lord in us is His Awesome Power.

The Lord our God parted the red sea and dried it up in the presence of the children of Israel, until they crossed over. He also dried up the waters of the Jordan before them until they had crossed over, <u>so that all the peoples of the earth may know the hand of the Lord, that it is mighty, and that you may fear the Lord your God for ever</u>"(Joshua 4: 23-24).

Job tells us that, "As for the Almighty, we cannot find Him; He is excellent in power, in judgment and abundant justice; He does not oppress, therefore men fear Him; He shows no partiality to any who are wise in heart" (Job.37:23-24).

Jesus taught His disciples the fear of God by saying, "My friends, do not be afraid of those who kill the body, and after that have no more that they can do. But I will show you whom you should fear: Fear Him who, after He has killed, has the power to cast into hell; yes I say to you, fear Him" (Luke 12:4-5).

Yes, because of the Lord's awesome power and authority, He ought to be feared, by standing in awe of Him, reverencing His name, and departing from evil. For it is written, "Let everyone who names the name of Christ depart from iniquity" (2 Timothy 2:19).

• The fifth motivating factor which should stimulate

the rightful fear of God in us is His Goodness.

The Psalmist David wrote, "Oh, how great is your goodness, which you have laid up for those who fear you, which you have prepared for those who trust in you in the presence of the sons of men!" (Psalms 31:19). It is the goodness of God that leads one to repentance; for this reason, God ought to be revered.

That is, love and respect deeply, honor greatly, show reverence, and stand in awe of Him. The prophet Samuel said, "I will teach you the good and right way. Only fear the Lord, and serve Him in truth with all your heart; for consider what great things He has done for you" (1Samuel 12:23-24).

Because of God's goodness, we are to fear the Lord our God, and serve Him, and to Him we should hold fast, and take oaths in His name. He is our praise, and He is our God, who has done for us great and awesome things which our eyes have seen.

* The sixth motivating factor which should stimulate the rightful fear of the Lord in us is "His Judgment."

For we must all appear before the judgment seat of Christ, that each one may receive the things done in the body, according to what he has done, whether good or bad. Knowing therefore, the terror of the Lord, we persuade men, to live in fear of Him.

Most people take into consideration, only the goodness of God, and failed to consider the severity of the Lord. We are to consider both the goodness and severity of the Lord, because on those who fell, and do not continue in his goodness, severity. But, towards those who continue in his goodness, kindness. We ought to bear in mind that, "the Lord God made the heavens and the earth by His great power and outstretched arm. There is nothing too hard for Him.

He shows loving kindness to thousands, and repays the iniquity of the fathers into the bosom of their children after them. The great and mighty God, whose name is the Lord of hosts, is great in counsel and mighty in work, for His eyes are open to all the ways of the sons of men, to give everyone according to his ways and according to the fruit of his doing" (Jeremiah 32:17-19).

The Lord is the true God; He is the living God and the everlasting King- At His wrath the earth will tremble, and the nations will not be able to abide His indignation" (Jeremiah 10:10).

We better take heed and listen to the angel who is flying in the midst of heaven with the everlasting gospel to preach to those who dwell on the earth- to every nation, tribe, tongue, and people- saying with a loud voice, "Fear God and give glory to Him, for the hour of His judgment has come; and worship Him who made heaven and earth, the sea and springs of water

We should also be joining the heavenly chorus and sing," We give you thanks, O Lord God almighty, the one who is and who was and who is to come, because You have taken Your great power and reigned. The nations were angry, and Your wrath has come, and the time of the dead (nations), that they should be judged, and that You should reward Your servants the prophets and the saints, and those who fear Your name, small and great, and should destroy those who destroy the earth" (Revelation 11:18).

Yes! If indeed we have proven that the Lord is gracious, let us fear Him and stand in Awe of Him, giving reverence to His name because of His Majesty-Sovereignty, His holiness, His forgiveness, His Power, His goodness, and His judgment.

2. If we have indeed proved that the Lord is gracious, it will be manifested in us as;-"New born babes desiring the pure milk of the word that we may grow thereby" (1Peter 2: 2).

The pure milk of the word is the pure undiluted word of righteousness. For, everyone who partakes only of milk is unskilled in the word of righteousness, for he is a babe.

The pure undiluted word of righteousness is subdivided into two parts.

A. Imputed righteousness.

This is our inherent state of holiness before God, because of the sacrifice of Jesus Christ. Therefore, we are to be found in Him (God), not having our own righteousness, which is from the law, but that which is through faith in Christ, the righteousness which is from God by faith" (Philippians 3:9).

God's righteousness has been imputed to man apart from works. Christ is the end of the law for righteousness, or the end of the law as the means of attaining righteousness.

God's righteousness is through faith in Jesus Christ, apart from the law, to all and on all who believe. (Romans 3:21-22). Righteousness and holiness, is the state in which man was begotten again, or re-created in Christ Jesus, according to God, at the resurrection of Jesus Christ.

But this imputed or inherent state of righteousness has to be exercised and developed, and be allowed to grow and bear fruit. This now brings us to the second integral part of righteousness.

B. Practical Righteousness.

Righteousness, similarly to holiness, requires one's concerted effort with the help of the Holy Spirit to develop. The same way we are instructed to be, as obedient children, not conforming ourselves to the former lusts as in our ignorance; but as He who called us is holy, we also be holy in all our conduct, because it is written, be holy, for I am holy so it is with regards to righteousness.

We are instructed saying, "If you know that He is righteous, you know that everyone who practices righteousness is born of Him" (1John 2:29).
In fact, as soon as one surrenders his/her life to Jesus Christ, and denounces sin (man's independent nature to think for him/herself, what is right and what is wrong, and walking according to the imagination of his own evil heart), he or she becomes a slave or servant of righteousness.

For it is written, "we are the one's slave whom we obey, whether of sin, unto death; or a slave of obedience to righteousness which leads to holiness, and at the end everlasting life. (Romans 6:16-22).

We are further told that, having been freed from sin {our independent nature}, you became slaves of righteousness. One who is a slave of sin, that is, one who obeys his own independent, sinful nature, and walks after the imagination of his own heart, which is evil above all things and desperately wicked, he /she is free in regards to righteousness.

Why? Because righteousness which is commonly defined as the keeping of God's commandments, is incomplete without our enslavement to the act of righteousness which is the only act that can bring about holiness and righteousness, and at the end everlasting life.

This act of righteous is the demonstration of the one act of righteousness which resulted in our justification, and brings life for all men. As it is written; "For whenever you eat this bread and drink this cup, you proclaim the Lord's death until he comes."

Therefore having been imputed with God's righteousness; has not negated the practice, or the obedience to the law and the act of righteousness. For we have been warned saying, "Little children, let no one deceive you. He who practices righteousness is righteous, just as He is righteous" (1John 3:7).

And therefore as obedient children, we should not desire to remain slaves to our independent, sinful nature, and following the dictates of our mind, but we are to rather become slaves of righteousness. That means obeying and practicing the law and act of righteousness to which we have been admonished saying; "Do not labor for the food which perishes, but for the food which endures to everlasting life, which the Son of Man will give to you; for on him has God the Father set his seal" (John 6:27).

Let us as new born babes, desire the pure milk of the word that we may grow thereby.

3. If indeed we have proven that the Lord is gracious, "We as living stones, are being built up into a spiritual house, a holy priesthood, to offer up spiritual sacrifices acceptable to God through Jesus Christ" (1Peter 2:5).

At the death of Jesus Christ, the Holy Spirit immersed or baptized humanity into the body which God had prepared for Christ, and united humanity with the body of Christ.

For it is written: "For by one Spirit we were all baptized into one body-whether Jews or Greeks, whether slaves or free-and have been made to drink into one Spirit" (1Corinthuans 12:13)

And, "God has set the members (every individual human being), each one of them, in the body just as He pleased" (1Corinthians 12:18).

The hope and expectancy of this unification is that, "If we have been united together in the likeness of His death, certainly we also shall be in the likeness of His resurrection, (that is, to have a glorified body at the resurrection) knowing that our old man was crucified with Him" (Romans 6:5-6).

But all depends on how one builds on the foundation, or develops and supports the body to which he/she has been united. For, "we are being built on the foundation of the apostles and prophets, Jesus Christ Himself being the chief cornerstone, in whom the whole building (or body), being joined together, grows into a holy temple in the Lord, in whom you (we) also are being built together for a habitation of God in the Spirit" (Ephesians 2:20-22).

It is this same temple or body (the body of Christ) that God has prepared for him that will become His bride. Hence this body to which humanity is united is, "not for sexual immorality but for the Lord and the Lord for the body" (1 Corinthians 6:13).

The reason for being crucified with Jesus Christ, and raised together with Him, is for the body of sin (our independent nature) to be done away with, and that we should no longer be slaves (servants) of sin". For, there is a way that seems right to a man, but its end is the way of death.

So then, as living stones, or members of a living organism (the body), we have been given the prerogative to choose our own building materials, or make our own provisions for the development and growth of the body. The materials for the construction of the temple, or the provisions for the growth and development of the body, are in two categories. In the area of construction, it is described as, the perishable, and the imperishable materials.

In pertaining to the body it is described as, sowing, and making provisions for the flesh, or sowing, and making provision for the Spirit.

Building with perishable materials, or sowing to the flesh will result in corruption. For, he who sows to the flesh shall of the flesh reap corruption.

For this reason we are admonished to, abstain from fleshly lusts which war against the soul, and flee from all harmful lusts which drown men in destruction and perdition. We are told that, every branch of the true vine, or every member of the body that does not bear fruit (the fruit of righteousness and true holiness in which they were created in Christ Jesus), the Father takes away.

If anyone does not abide in the state of the body in which they were united, he/she is cast out as a branch and is withered; and they gather them and throw them into the fire, and they are burned.

In like manner, if anyone builds on this foundation (the body of Christ to which we are united), with gold, silver, precious stones, wood hay, straw, each one's work will become manifest; for the Day will declare it, because it will be revealed by fire; and the fire will test each one's work, of what sort it is.

If anyone's work which he has built on it (the body of Christ) endures, he will receive a reward (permanent existence in the body, Everlasting life, immortality). On the other hand, "if anyone's work is burned, he will suffer loss (detachment from the body); but he himself will be saved yet so as through fire" (1Corinthians 3:12-15).

The imperishable materials with which we are to construct our temple on the foundation are: Faith, Righteousness, knowledge, temperance , perseverance, godliness-holiness, brotherly kindness and love. They are to be diligently pursued, without spot and blameless until our Lord Jesus Christ appears.

Hence we are admonished by the Apostle Paul saying, "But you O man of God, flee these things (youthful and harmful lusts which drowns men into destruction and perdition), and pursue righteousness, godliness, faith, love, patience, gentleness."

He further urged us by saying, "I urge you in the sight of God who gives life to all things, and before Christ Jesus who witnessed the good confession before Pontius Pilate, that you keep this command without spot, blameless until our Lord Jesus Christ's appearing" (1Timothy 6:11-14). We have to build on the foundation which has been freely given to us

4. If indeed we have proved that the Lord is gracious, we will strive to remain a part of his body, by building on righteousness and perfecting holiness in the fear of the Lord, and pursuing the other qualities that go along with it.

Salvation although it is a free gift, has to be exercised with much fear and trembling, and when expressing our gratitude we should besides ourselves, bring along words and a gift in our hand. For it is written, "O Israel return to the Lord your God, for you have stumbled because of your iniquity; take words with you, and return to the Lord. Say to Him, take away all iniquity; receive us graciously, for we will offer the sacrifices of our lips" (Hosea 14:1-2).

We are admonished saying; "Therefore, through Jesus, let us continually offer to God a sacrifice of praise, the fruit of our lips, giving thanks to his name, and do not forget to do good and to share with others, for with such sacrifices God is well pleased" (Hebrews 13:15-16).

5. If indeed we have tasted that the Lord is gracious, our gifts and offerings must be acceptable, and well pleasing in His sight.

The Lord our God as the Father and Master, deserves our highest honor and reverence. As it is written, "A son honors his father and a servant his master. If then I am the Father where is my honor? And if I am a Master, where is my reverence? Says the Lord of hosts to you priests who despise my name: yet you say, in what way have we despised your name? (Malachi 1:6).

Remember, in the New Testament dispensation, those who have accepted the Lord as Father and Master, "are a chosen generation, a royal priesthood, a holy nation, His own special people, that they may proclaim the praises of Him who called them out of darkness into His marvelous light" (1Peter 2:9).

They are also, "As living stones, are being built up a spiritual house, a holy priesthood to offer up spiritual sacrifices acceptable to God through Jesus Christ" (1Peter 2:5). We are cautioned therefore saying, "And when you offer the blind as a sacrifice, is it not evil? And when you offer the lame and sick, is it not evil? Offer it then to your Governor! Would he be pleased with you? Would he accept you favorably? Says the Lord of hosts!

 But now entreat God's favor, that He may be gracious to us. While this is being done by your hands (offering inferior and profane things to God) will He accept you favorably? Says the Lord of hosts" (Malachi 1:8-9).

God is not willing to accept any profane and unacceptable sacrifice brought before Him, because He says, "Cursed be the deceiver who has in his flock a male and makes a vow, but sacrifices to the Lord what is blemished. For I am a Great King, and my name is to be feared among the nations" (Malachi 1:14).

The only perfect sacrifice one can offer to the Father that will satisfies Him is, the offering He considers as, "My offering, my food for my offerings made by fire as a sweet aroma to me" (Numbers 28:2).

This sweet aroma is the perfect sacrifice of His Son, represented by the bread and the wine, and one should be careful to offer it to him at their appointed time.

When Christ came into the world, he said: "Sacrifices and offerings, burnt offerings and sin offerings you did not desire, nor were you pleased with them" (although the law required them to be made). Then he said, "Here I am, I have come to do your will." He sets aside the first to establish the second. And by that will, we have been made holy through the sacrifice of the body of Jesus Christ once for all" (Hebrews 10:8-10).

The first which was set aside was animal and food sacrifices which could not take away sins. And the second that has been established is the sacrifice of the sinless body of Christ on the cross, and represented by the ordinance of the bread and wine, which Jesus Christ instituted prior to his death.

The reason why we have been urged by the mercies of God to, "Offer our bodies as living sacrifices, holy and pleasing to God, which is our spiritual act of worship", it is in order to offer to the Lord his offering, which is our main objective for our calling as a nation of priests.

6. If indeed we have proven that the Lord is gracious, The sacrifices that we offer must be offered in the spirit of rejoicing.

Anything that we give to the Lord must be of a cheerful heart, for thus says the Lord; "If you keep your feet from breaking the Sabbath, and from doing as you please on my holy day, if you call the Sabbath a delight and the Lord's holy day honorable, and if you honor it by not going your own way, and not doing as you please, or speaking idle words, then you will find your joy in the Lord, and I will cause you to ride on the heights of the land, and to feast on the inheritance of your father Jacob.' The mouth of the Lord has spoken" (Isaiah 58:13-14).

God loves a cheerful giver who shows appreciation to what the Lord has done, as shown in Psalms 107: 21-22 which reads; " Oh that men would give thanks to the Lord for his goodness and for his wonderful works to the children of men! Let them sacrifice the sacrifices of thanksgiving and declare His works with rejoicing." And in 2 Corinthians 9:7 states; "Let each one give, as he purposes in his heart, not grudgingly or of necessity; for God loves a cheerful giver!"

Remember that, a sacrifice of thanksgiving is, of one's own volition, offered in love, gratitude, and in appreciation for what the Lord has done, and continues to do. It is not offered based on any law, obligation, compulsion, or coercion. But it is based entirely on obedience to an established principle ordained by God, as the way of life, which one has voluntarily choose to follow.

7. If indeed we have proven that the Lord is gracious, we must pay our vows.

Promises are normally made to the Lord, when we have proved his goodness, either whilst we are in trouble or after delivering us from calamities, and after everything is won, we tend to forget our vows and promises. We are therefore instructed saying, "Offer to God thanksgiving, and pay your vows to the most high. Call upon me in the day of trouble, I will deliver you, and you shall glorify me" (Psalms 50:14-15).

However, the admonition is, "When you make a vow to God, do not delay to pay it; For He has no pleasure in fools. Pay what you have vowed. It is better not to vow than to vow and not pay" (Ecclesiastes 5:4-5).

A sacrifice of thanksgiving is offered in the following ways:-

a. Prayer:

It is stated "Let my prayer be set before you as an incense: the lifting up of my hands as the evening sacrifice" (Psalms 141:2).

The prayers of the saints, ascends before God from the hands of an angel as the burning of incense. For it is written, "An angel having a golden censer, came and stood at the altar; And he was given much incense, that he should offer it with the prayers of all the saints upon the golden altar which was before the throne. And the smoke of the incense, with the prayers of the saints, ascends before God from the angel's hand" (Revelation 8:3-4, 5:8).

Such sacrifices should be offered without ceasing. We are instructed to "rejoice always, pray without ceasing, in everything give thanks; for this is the will of God in Christ Jesus for you. Do not quench the Spirit" (1Thessalonians 5:16-19).

b. Worship:

We are to continually offer the food for the Lord's offerings made by fire as a sweet aroma to him, which is the heart and core of Worship. For thus says the Lord in the book of Leviticus chapter 23: verses 37 and 38; "These are the Lord's appointed feasts, which you are to proclaim as sacred assemblies **for bringing offerings** made to the Lord by (zeal) fire – the burnt offering is figurative to Jesus Christ the Lamb of God; its grain offerings is the body of Jesus Christ in the form of unleavened bread, and its drink offering, is the blood of Christ in the form of wine.

This offering is of paramount importance in every worship

service. It is besides or in addition to the Lord's Sabbaths, in addition to our gifts and whatsoever we have vowed and all the free will offerings the fruit of our lips, and giving of thanks which we give to the Lord. In addition, the Lord has appointed specific times when we should appear before Him, and should not appear before Him empty-handed.

c. Acts of righteousness

It is clearly stated that "All of us have become like one who is unclean, and all our righteous acts are like filthy rags" (Isaiah 64:6); Nevertheless we must not forget to do what is good and to share, for with such sacrifices God is well pleased" (Hebrews 13:16).

We are to offer the sacrifice of righteousness, which is to proclaim the Lord's death, Loving God by keeping His commandments, and loving our neighbors, as ourselves.

8. If indeed we have proved that the Lord is gracious, His graciousness will also be manifested in our lives. For, of His fullness we have all received, and grace for grace.

Grace is a terminology that is frequently used in the religious circle, but unfortunately it is misapplied by many. Grace is God's unmerited favor, mercy and compassion which he bestowed upon man for a distinctive purpose which is to show appreciation and giving back to him. Grace is reciprocal.

Grace however stands between two extremes.

1. Legalism

The extremity of the rough and turbulent waters of legalism, where God's grace have been received in vain by those who attempt to be justified by the works of the law, and have unfortunately fallen from grace. Because, as it is written, "If anything is by grace, then it is no longer of works;

otherwise grace is no longer grace. And if anything is of works, it is no longer grace; otherwise work is no longer work" (Romans 11:6).

2. Liberalism

The extremity of the calm, placid, but extremely toxic waters of liberalism, where the grace of God has been turned into a license for disobedience, and even denying the only Lord God and our Lord Jesus Christ, by those who are using their liberty as an opportunity for the flesh, and as a pretext for evil.

The grace of God is simply his unmerited, undeserved favor, compassion, and mercy which he bestowed upon humanity without their help and participation, for their ultimate salvation.

This undeserved favor of grace is descriptive of:-

•   God's Favor

The favor of his only Begotten Son who reconciled us to the Father even when we were dead in trespasses and sins.

•   His forgiving mercy

By forgiving us of the sins of the past, and being faithful and just to forgive us our sins and to cleanse us of all unrighteousness if we confess our sins.

•   His gift of eternal life

The medium by which we can grope for him and find him, and come to know him, the only true God and Jesus Christ whom he has sent.

•   His divine gifts and talents

His divine power which has given to us all things that pertain to life and godliness, through the knowledge of him who called us by glory and virtue. He has given to all without exception, life, breath and all things.

- The Gospel

The medium by which we can grow in grace and in the knowledge of our Lord and Savior Jesus Christ. Because without faith it is impossible to please God, and faith comes by hearing, and hearing by the word of God.

Grace therefore establishes the foundation by which man can serve God, without his own input and involvement, so that no one can boast. As it is written; "But when the kindness and love of God our Savior toward man appeared, he saved us, not because of righteous things we had done, but because of his mercy, he saved us through the washing of rebirth and renewal by the Holy Spirit, whom he poured out on us generously through Jesus Christ our Savior" (Titus 3:4-6).

It is by grace we have been, and are being saved, through faith (hearing the word of God and believing), and this is not from ourselves, it is the gift of God, not by works, so that no one can boast.

But the objective for God's grace is for us as God's workmanship, created in Christ Jesus for the purpose of good works, which God prepared in advance for us to do.

We have been saved by grace so that those who have trusted in God by hearing and believing his word may be careful to devote themselves to doing what is good. These things are excellent and profitable for everyone.

Doing what is good is not according to each man's imagination of what is right and wrong, but according to the good which has been prepared in advance for us to do.

Because, there is a way which seems right to a man, but the

end thereof is the way of death.

Therefore being justified by grace does not nullify, or make obsolete the Way of life which has been ordained for man to live For it is written: "What then? Shall we sin because we are not under law but under grace? By no means! Do you not know that when you yield yourselves to anyone as obedient slaves, you are slaves of the one whom you obey, either slaves of sin, which leads to death, or slaves of obedience to the law of God, which leads to righteousness" (Romans 6:15-16).

God has ordained one Way of life for man to follow. He said, "I gave them my statutes and made known to them my judgments, which, if a man does, he shall live, aspire, flourish by them" (Leviticus 18:5, Ezekiel 20:11, 13).

The Lord said to Moses, "One ordinance shall be for you of the congregation and for the stranger who sojourns with you, an ordinance forever throughout your generations; as you are, so shall the stranger be before the Lord. One law and one custom shall be for you and for the stranger who sojourns with you" (Numbers 15:15-16).

Man is a slave to either the independent, insatiable desires of the flesh called sin, or a slave to obedience to the law of righteousness.

One should not misconstrued the statement, "For Christ is the end of the law **for righteousness** to everyone who believes," to mean that he is the end of the law **of righteousness** to everyone who believes. For it is written, "Do we then make void the law through faith? Certainly not! On the contrary, we establish the law" (Romans 3:31).

The reality is, having been made free from the power and master of sin, one becomes a slave to righteousness; and having been set free from sin, and having become slaves of

God, one has his fruit to holiness, and the end everlasting life.

In other words, obedience to righteousness produces holiness, and holiness culminates into everlasting life. When one is a slave to sin [man's sinful nature, the life in the flesh] he is free or far removed in regards to righteousness. In like manner, when one is a slave to righteousness (obeying the laws of God, living in according to the Spirit) he is free or far removed from sin (doing what is right in his/her own eyes).

One must not negate practical righteousness which leads to holiness because of imputed righteousness as we have been admonished saying, "Dear children, do not let anyone lead you astray. He who practices righteousness is righteous just as he Jesus Christ is righteous" (1John 3:7).

We have also been warned saying, "Whoever breaks one of the least of these commandments, and teaches men so, shall be called least in the kingdom of heaven; but whoever does and teaches them, he shall be called great in the kingdom of heaven" (Matthew 5:19).

On the other hand the strict observers of the law ought not to impose their strict observance to the law as though one's salvation or eternal life hinges on them. Both extremes are wrong and dangerous.

The law is not made for a righteous person, but for the lawless and insubordinate, for the ungodly and for sinners, for the unholy and profane, for murderers of fathers and murderers of mothers, for man slayers, for fornicators, for sodomites, for kidnappers, for liars, for perjurers, and any other thing that is contrary to sound doctrine" (1Timothy 1:9-10).

The reason why the law is not for the righteous man is

because, the law as the tutor, guardian, school master, spiritual mirror, that reveals sin, has already pointed him to Christ, and since he has believed, he is now living within the confines of the law, by faith.

The purpose for the grace of God is to cause thanksgiving to overflow to the glory of God. Because what we are is a gift from God, and what we become is a gift to God. For this reason we should not forsake the assembling of ourselves together especially on the days he has specifically ordained to worship and reverence him as the one and only true God.

For this is what the Lord says; "Keep my Sabbaths and reverence my sanctuary. I am the Lord" (Leviticus 19:30; 26:2). This is how those who have turned the grace of God into licentiousness have denied the one and only Lord God, and our Lord Jesus Christ who said, "...The Son of Man is Lord even of the Sabbath" (Mark 2:27).

Nevertheless, one has no right to command, coerce, or compel another to do what has been taught. Because, "The grace of God that bring salvation has appeared to all men, teaching us to say 'No' to ungodliness, and worldly passions, and to live self controlled, upright and godly in this present age, while we wait for the blessed hope – the glorious appearing of our great God and Savior, Jesus Christ, who gave himself for us to redeem us from all wickedness and to purify for himself a people that are his very own, eager to do what is good" (Titus 2:11-14).

The eagerness to do what is good is derived not from law, command, or coercion, but by faith in what Jesus Christ has done for us and the love we have for him. As it is written, "If you love me keep my commandments." And our eagerness to seek first the kingdom of God and his righteousness.

We are to let the grace of God cause thanksgiving to

overflow to the glory of God:

Because of his grace we are to, "Come, let us sing for joy to the Lord: let us shout aloud to the Rock of our salvation, let us come before him with thanksgiving and extol him with music and song. For the Lord is the great God, the great King above all gods, in his hands are the depths of the earth, and the mountain peaks belong to him. The sea is his, for he made it, and his hands formed the dry land.

"Let us come and bow down in worship. Let us kneel before the Lord our Maker; for he is our God, and we are the people of his pasture, the flock under his care. Today, if you will hear his voice, do not harden your hearts" (Psalms 95:1-7).

We express our gratitude to God by appearing before him on the days he has appointed as his festivals, ascribing to him the glory that is due to his name, and offering to him his food for his offering, which is the new and better way by which we can now draw near to him, in a perfect, blameless, and irreproachable state. All praise to our God for his manifold wisdom.

Chapter Seven

Jesus Christ the Chief Cornerstone

Christianity is undoubtedly portrayed in scriptures as a construction work, were each individual has been given a solid foundation on which to build his/her eternal destiny.

The apostle Paul alluded to this perception by stating; "According to the grace of God given to me like a skilled master builder, I laid a foundation and another man is building upon it. Let each man take care how he builds upon it. For no other foundation can any one lay than that which is laid, which is Jesus Christ" (1Corinthians 3:10-11).

In another instance the apostle Paul described believers as, "Members of the household of God, built upon the foundation of the apostles and prophets, and Christ himself being the corner stone in whom the whole structure is joined together and grows into a holy temple in the Lord; in whom believers also are built into it for a dwelling place of God in the Spirit" (Ephesians 2:19-22).

The apostle Peter echoed similar sentiments by urging all believers to, "Come to Christ, to that living stone, rejected by men but in God's sight chosen and precious; and like living stones built yourselves into a spiritual house, to be a holy priesthood, to offer spiritual sacrifices acceptable to God through Jesus Christ" (1Peter 2: 4-5).

The job description of those who are called is clear with absolutely no ambiguity, and there is only one hope for this calling, and the reward is based on how one pursues that hope. It is only if the work which any man has built on this foundation survives, that he will receives a reward, because the quality of every man's work will be revealed by fire, and will test every man's work of what sort it is.

Every structure is supported and joined together by the

cornerstone, and in constructing the spiritual house one must assure him/herself that as living stone he/she is properly integrated, amalgamated, and well supported by the four corner stones of the spiritual temple, if not the slightest turbulence can cause a rift between the living stones and the cornerstone.

The four cornerstones of the spiritual temple on which we are integrated and amalgamated, in order to build our own spiritual structure are:-

1. **Jesus Christ our Wisdom and Power**

Jesus Christ is the cornerstone of our wisdom and power because according to the apostle Paul, "We do however speak a message of wisdom among the mature, but not the wisdom of this age or of the rulers of this age, who are coming to nothing; No, we speak of God's secret wisdom, a wisdom that has been hidden and that God destined for our glory before time began.'

"None of the rulers of this age understood it, for if they had they would not have crucified the Lord of glory. However, as it is written; "no eye has seen, no ear has heard, no mind has conceived what God has prepared for those who love him, but God has revealed it to us by his Spirit" (1Corinthians 2:6-9).

What exactly is that secret wisdom and power of God which he destined for our glory?

The secret wisdom and power of God which he destined for our glory is, Jesus Christ who because the children have flesh and blood, he too shared in their humanity so that by his death he might destroy him who holds the power of death – that is the devil – and free those who all their lives were held in slavery by their fear of death, so he yielded his life for atonement for sin, and open the life gate that all may go in.

According to the apostle Paul "The message of the cross is foolishness to those who are perishing, but to us who are being saved it is the power of God. For it is written; "I will destroy the wisdom of the wise: the intelligence of the intelligent I will frustrate."

He then posed the following questions; "Where is the wise man? Where is the Scholar? Where is the philosopher of this age? Has not God made foolishness the wisdom of the world? For since in the wisdom of God the world did not know God through wisdom: it pleased God through the foolishness of what we preach, to save those who believe" (1 Corinthians 1:20-21).

How exactly do we preach the message of the cross, which is to those who are perishing foolishness, and to those who are being saved the power of God?

To preach the message of the cross is not just a verbal exercise, it involves a demonstration of the message of the cross. The secret mystery which was revealed to the apostle Paul is this; "For I received from the Lord what I also passed on to you: The Lord Jesus, on the night he was betrayed, took bread, and when he had given thanks, he broke it and said, 'This is my body, which is for you; do this in remembrance of me." In the same way, after supper he took the cup, saying, "This cup is the new covenant in my blood; do this, whenever you drink it, in remembrance of me. For whenever you eat this bread and drink this cup, you proclaim the Lord's death until he comes" (1Corinthians 11:23-26).

The apostle Paul said; "Jews demand miraculous signs and Greeks look for wisdom, but we preach Christ crucified: a stumbling block to Jews and foolishness to Gentiles, but to those whom God has called, both Jews and Greeks, Christ the power of God and the wisdom of God. For the foolishness of God is wiser than men, and the weakness of

God is stronger than men" (1Corinthians 1:18-25).

We are integrated into this corner stone in view of God's mercy, by offering our bodies as living sacrifices, holy and pleasing to God (as priests in order to offer to the Lord his food for his offering) this is our spiritual act of worship.

The church has been given the responsibility to make known to the rulers and authorities in the heavenly places (Satan and his demons) the manifold wisdom of God, which for ages past was kept hidden in God. The apostle Paul clarified this by saying; "To me, though I am the very least of all the saints, this grace was given, to preach to the Gentiles the unsearchable riches of Christ, and to make all men see what is the plan of the mystery hidden for ages in God who created all things.'

This mystery the apostle Paul said, "Was according to the eternal purpose which God has realized in Christ Jesus our Lord, in whom we have boldness and confidence of access through our faith in him" (Ephesians 3:8-12).

The apostle Paul endorsed the source of our boldness and confidence to the Father by saying; "Therefore, brethren, since we have confidence to enter the most holy place by the blood of Jesus, by a new and living way opened for us through the curtain, that is, his flesh, and since we have a great priest over the house of God, let us draw near to God with a sincere heart in full assurance of faith, having our hearts sprinkled to cleanse us from a guilty conscience and having our bodies washed with pure water" (Hebrews 10:19-22).

2. Jesus Christ Our Righteousness

Jesus Christ is the cornerstone of our righteousness because his death fulfilled the righteous requirements of the law, by paying the penalty of sin in full, which is death, and conferred his righteousness to all those who receive God's abundant provision of grace and of the gift of righteousness, and will reign in life through the one man Jesus Christ .

As the result of this one act of righteousness, justification which brings life, came for all men. As the scripture clearly states; "But now, the righteousness of God apart from law has been made known, to which the law and the prophet testify. This righteousness from God; comes through faith in Jesus Christ to all who believe" (Romans 5: 17-19; 3: 21-22).

This righteousness has not only been imputed, but has to be practiced as well, because we have been admonished saying; "you have been set free from sin and have become slaves to righteousness.' And, "Little children, let no one deceive you. He who practices righteousness is righteousness just as he is righteous" (Romans 6: 18; 1John 3:7).

This act of righteousness is the only righteous act that can produce holiness, because, all of man's righteousness is as filthy rags before God

This act of righteousness is to become slaves to God as priests, to offer to him his food for his offerings at its appointed time, and having become slaves to God, the benefit we reap leads to holiness, and the result is everlasting life.

3. **Jesus Christ our Sanctification**

Jesus Christ is the corner stone of our sanctification as a result of his resurrection from the dead, and his appointment as High Priest who lives for ever and has a permanent priesthood, and is able to save completely those who come to God through him, because he always lives to intercede for them.

Such a High Priest meets our need – one who is holy, blameless, pure, and set apart from sinners, exalted above the heavens. Both righteousness and holiness (sanctification) is a state which has been conferred upon believers because of the death and resurrection of Jesus Christ. Hence we are admonished to "Put on the new man, created to be like God in true righteousness and holiness" (Ephesians 4: 24).

Therefore, as living stones we are integrated into the cornerstone of holiness by God the Father who has blessed us in Christ with every spiritual blessing in the heavenly places, even as he chose us in him before the foundation of the world that we should be holy and blameless before him.

This spiritual state has to be perfected by cleansing ones self from every defilement of body and spirit, and making holiness perfect in the fear of God.

This necessitates our separation from everything that defiles as we have been instructed saying; "Do not be yoked together with unbelievers. For what do righteousness and wickedness have in common? Or what fellowship can light have with darkness? What harmony is there between Christ and Belial? What does a believer have in common with an unbeliever? What agreement is there between the temple of God and idols? For, we are the temple of the living God.'

"As God has said, "I will live with them and walk among them, and I will be their God, and they will be my people. Therefore come out from them and be separate, says the Lord. Touch no unclean thing, and I will receive you. I will be a Father to you, and you will be my sons and daughters, says the Lord Almighty" (2 Corinthians 6:14-18).

Christ the cornerstone of our sanctification has called his people out of the world, and prayed to the Father on their behalf saying; "I have given them your word and the world has hated them, for they are not of the world anymore than I am of the world. My prayer is not that you take them out of the world but to protect them from the evil one. They are not of the world, even as I am not of it. Sanctify them by the truth; your word is truth. As you sent me into the world, I have sent them into the world. For them I sanctify myself, that they too may be truly sanctified" (John 17:14-19).

It is also by the authority of Christ our sanctification that Paul issued a letter to the church saying; "I have written to you in my letter not to associate with sexually immoral people – not at all meaning the people of this world who are immoral, or the greedy and swindlers, or idolaters.

"In that case you would have to leave this world. But now I am writing to you that you must not associate with anyone who calls himself a brother but is sexually immoral or greedy, an idolater or a slanderer, a drunkard or a swindler, with such a man do not even eat."

"What business is it of mine to judge those outside the church? God will judge those outside. Expel the wicked man from among you" (1Corinthians 5:9-13).

A messenger of Christ our sanctification has issued a warning saying; "Come out of her, my people so that you will not share in her sins, so that you will not receive any of her plagues" (Revelation 18:4).

4. Jesus Christ our Redemption

Jesus Christ is the cornerstone of our redemption because only in him we have redemption through his blood the forgiveness of sins. God has delivered us from the dominion of darkness and transferred us to the kingdom of his beloved Son, in whom we have redemption, the forgiveness of sins.

Redemption is not a one time process as it is commonly assumed, it is an ongoing process. The one time process of redemption is, once and for all there is now an offering that can present the worshiper holy, perfect, and blameless in the presence of God.

It is made absolutely clear that without the shedding of blood there is no forgiveness, and no one can say that I have no sin, or have not sinned. Therefore, "If we claim to be without sin we deceive ourselves and the truth is not in us. If we claim we have not sinned we make him out to be a liar and his word has no place in our lives."

But, if any body does sin, we have an advocate with the Father Jesus Christ the righteous. He is the atoning sacrifice for our sins, and not only for ours, but also for the sins of the whole world. If we confess our sins, he is faithful and just and will forgive us our sins and purify us from all unrighteousness. It is the blood of Christ that (not purified as in the past, but as an ongoing process) purifies us from all sins.

It is stated quite categorically that the life of the flesh is in the blood: and God has given it to us upon the altar to make atonement for our souls; for it is the blood that makes atonement for one's life. Therefore, the cup of the New Covenant which was instituted on the night before Jesus Christ was led to be crucified and became effective after his death, was part and parcel of the plan of the mystery hidden in ages in God.

According to the scriptures, a testament is in force only when some body has died; it never takes effect while the one who made it is living. Therefore the cup of the new covenant of Christ's blood became effective after his death and that was all part of God's redemption plan for man.

The corner stone of our spiritual structure therefore is, Jesus Christ coming in the flesh, his death and resurrection, and his appointment as the eternal High Priest, and his flesh and blood as the food for God's offering as the redemption price for our sins. For thus it is written; "God is the source of our life in Jesus Christ, whom he made our wisdom, our righteousness and sanctification and redemption; therefore, as it is written, "Let him who boasts, boast of the Lord" (1Corinthians 1:30-31).

It is the lack of, and improper discernment of the body and blood of Jesus Christ that is the cause of the believer's weakness, sickness and premature death. We should therefore learn how to build our spiritual house on the chief corner stone, in view of God's mercy, to offer our bodies as living sacrifices (as priests), holy and pleasing to God, which is our spiritual act of worship.

It is the requirement for "Priests to be holy to their God, and must not profane the name of their God, because they present the offerings made to the Lord by fire, the food of their God, they are to be holy. Priests are holy to their God and should be regarded as holy, because they offer up the food of their God. The Lord says "Consider them holy, because I the Lord am holy – I who make you holy" (Leviticus 21: 6, 8).

Our admonition is to; "Come to him, the living Stone, rejected by men but chosen by God and precious to him. You also, like living stones, are being built into a spiritual house to be a holy priesthood, offering spiritual sacrifices acceptable to God through Jesus Christ.'

It is stated that, "People stumble because they disobey the message, which is also what they were destined for..." " But you (the believer), are a chosen people, a royal priesthood, a holy nation, a people belonging to God, that you may declare the praises of him who called you out of darkness into his marvelous light. Once we were not a people, but now we are the people of God; once we had not received mercy, but now we have received mercy" (1Peter 2: 5, 9).

All praise to the God and Father of our Lord Jesus Christ, who has blessed us in the heavenly realms with every spiritual blessing in Christ, who chose us in him before the creation of the world to be holy and blameless in his sight. In love he predestined us to be adopted as his sons through Jesus Christ in accordance with his pleasure and will, to the praise of his glorious grace, which he has given us in the one he loves, in whom we have redemption through his blood, the forgiveness of sins, in accordance with the riches of God's grace that he lavished on us with all wisdom and understanding.'

"And he made known to us the mystery of his will according to his good pleasure, which he purposed in Christ, to be put into effect when the times will have reached their fulfillment" (Ephesians 1:3-10).

I think the time has reached its fulfillment. Therefore as obedient children, let us not conform ourselves to the evil desires we had when we lived in ignorance, but just as he who called us is holy, so let us be holy in all we do; for it is written: "Be holy, because I am holy" (1Peter 1:16).

The Mystery of God's Will

In several passages of scripture the apostle Paul made reference to God's mystery, his secret wisdom which was kept secret for ages from other generations, but has now been revealed to his saints.

The Apostle wrote; "In him we have redemption through his blood, the forgiveness of sins, according to the riches of his grace which he made to abound toward us in all wisdom and understanding, having made known to us the mystery of his will, according to his good pleasure which he purposed in himself" (Ephesians 1:7-9).

This mystery is God's secret wisdom which he ordained before the ages for our glory, which none of the rulers of this age knew; for had they known, they would not have crucified the Lord of Glory.

The Mystery of God's Will Revealed

This mystery which is for our glory, and was kept secret and not revealed to the sons of men in other ages has now been revealed to us, it is the redemption we have through the blood of Jesus for the forgiveness of sins.

According to the apostle Paul we should not be ashamed of the testimony of our Lord which in effect is, "For there is one Mediator between God and men, the Man Jesus Christ, who gave himself a ransom for all, to be testified in due times" (1Timothy 2:5).

The gospel according to the power of God is that, "God has saved us and called us with a holy calling, not according to our works, but according to his own purpose and grace which was given to us in Christ Jesus before time began, but has now been revealed by the appearing of our Savior Jesus Christ, who has abolished death and brought life and immortality to light through the gospel" (2 Timothy 1:9-10).

The gospel reveals the way our Savior Jesus Christ abolished death, and brought life and immortality to light, so that no one is excusable.

Jesus said; "I am the bread of life. Your fathers ate the manna in the wilderness, and are dead. This is the bread which comes down from heaven, and one may eat of eat and not die. I am the living bread which came down from heaven. If anyone eats of this bread, he will live forever; and the bread that I shall give is my flesh, which I shall give for the life of the world.'

Even after the Jews expressed their disgust and disbelief at Jesus' statement, He reiterated and affirmed his statement by saying; "Most assuredly, I say to you, unless you eat the flesh of the Son of Man and drink his blood, you have no life in you. Whoever eats my flesh and drinks my blood has eternal life, and I will raise him up at the last day. For my flesh is food indeed, and my blood is drink indeed.'

"He who eats my flesh and drinks my blood abides in me, and I in him. As the living Father sent me, and I live because of the Father, so he who feeds on me will live because of me. This is the bread which came down from heaven – not as your fathers ate the manna, and are dead. He who eats this bread will live for ever" (John 6:48-58).

This mystery was revealed to the apostle Paul who wrote; "I Paul, the prisoner of Jesus Christ for you Gentiles – if indeed you have heard of the dispensation of the grace of God which was given to me for you, how that by revelation he made known to me the mystery (as I wrote before in few words, by which when you read, you may understand my knowledge in the mystery of Christ), which in other ages was not made known to the sons of men, as it has now been revealed by the Spirit to his holy apostles and prophets; that the Gentiles should be fellow heirs, of the same body, and partakers of his promise in Christ through the gospel, of which I became a minister according to the gift of the grace of God given to me by the effective working of his power" (Ephesians 3:1-7).

Gentiles are now fellow heirs of the same body, and partakers of God's promise in Christ through the gospel which speaks in this wise; "I speak as to wise men; judge for your-selves what I say. The cup of blessing which we bless, is it not the communion of the blood of Christ? The bread which we break, is it not the communion of the body of Christ? For we, being many, are one bread and one body; for we all partake of that one bread" (1Corithians 10:16-17).

What was revealed to the apostle Paul is the way to; "Open the eyes of the Gentiles and turn them from darkness to light, and from the power of Satan to God, that they may receive forgiveness of sins and an inheritance among those who are sanctified by faith in Jesus Christ" (Acts 26:18).

The apostle Paul declared the mystery to the church by stating; "For I have received from the Lord that which I also delivered to you; that the Lord Jesus on the same night in which he was betrayed took bread; and when he had given thanks, he broke it and said, "Take, eat; this is my body which is broken for you; do this in remembrance of me." In the same manner he also took the cup after supper, saying, "This cup is the new covenant in my blood, this do as often as you drink it, in remembrance of me." For as often as you eat this bread and drink this cup, you proclaim the Lord's death till he comes" (1Corinthians 11:23-26).

The bread and the wine are figurative to the manna and the rock which sustained the children of Israel during their journey in the wilderness. "They ate manna forty years, until they came to an inhabited land; they ate manna until they came to the border of the land of Canaan" (Exodus 16:35).

We also, are being miraculously fed with the true bread from heaven, as we journey through the wilderness of sin until Christ comes.

The Intent of the Mystery of God's Will

The intent of this mystery is for the church to demonstrate the manifold wisdom of God to the principalities and powers in the heavenly places, and to have access to the Father with all boldness and confidence through faith in Jesus Christ.

The apostle Paul wrote; "To me, who am less than the least of all the saints, this grace was given, that I should preach among the Gentiles the unsearchable riches of Christ, and to make all people see what is the fellowship of the mystery, which from the beginning of the ages has been hidden in God who created all things through Jesus Christ;'

"To the intent that now the manifold wisdom of God might be made known by the church to the principalities and powers in the heavenly places, according to the eternal purpose which he accomplished in Christ Jesus our Lord, in whom we have boldness and access with confidence through faith in him" (Ephesians 3:8-9).

We are admonished by the apostle Paul to hold fast to our confession. He said; "Therefore, brethren, having boldness to enter the Holiest by the blood of Jesus, by a new and living way which he consecrated for us, through the veil, that is, his flesh, and having a High Priest over the house of God, let us draw near with a true heart in full assurance of faith, having our hearts sprinkled from an evil conscience and our bodies washed with pure water, let us hold fast the confession of our hope without wavering, for he who promised is faithful.'

"And let us consider one another in order to stir up love and good works, not forsaking the assembling of ourselves together, as is the manner of some, but exhorting one another, and so much the more as you see the Day approaching" (Hebrews 10:19-25).

The objective of this mystery is to present the worshiper before God in a holy, blameless, perfect and irreproachable state. It is the food of God's offerings which satisfies his will. He said to Moses; "Command the children of Israel and say to them, my offering, my food for my offerings made by fire as a sweet aroma to me, you shall be careful to offer to me at their appointed time' (Numbers 28:2).

God ordained specific times to offer to him his offering, it is besides or in addition to everything else one may wish to offer to the Lord. He said; "These are the feasts of the Lord which you shall proclaim to be holy convocations, _**to offer an offering**_ made by fire to the Lord, a burnt offering and a grain offering, a sacrifice and drink offerings, everything on its day – besides the Sabbaths of the Lord, besides your gifts, besides all your vows, and besides all your free will offerings which you give to the Lord" (Leviticus 23: 37-38).

This offering is the offering which Jesus Christ as our High Priest, is appointed to offer to the Father on behalf of our sins, and since "He continues forever, he has an unchangeable priesthood, and therefore he is also able to save to the uttermost those who come to the Father through him, since he ever lives to make intercession for them..'

"For such a High Priest was fitting for us, who is holy, harmless, undefiled, separate from sinners, and has become higher than the heavens; who does not need daily, as those high priests, to offer up sacrifices, first for his own sins and then for the people's, for this he did once for all when he offered up himself" (Hebrews 7:24-27).

Appreciation of the Mystery of God's Will

We need to show our appreciation of this mystery by being obedient to the faith. In rendering his benediction the apostle Paul said; "Now to him who is able to establish you according to my gospel and the preaching of Jesus Christ, according to the revelation of the mystery which was kept secret since the world began, but now has been made manifest, and by the prophetic scriptures has been made known to all nations, according to the commandment of the everlasting God, for obedience to the faith – to God, alone wise, be glory through Jesus Christ forever. Amen.'

Because of the apostle Paul's deep understanding of this mystery he wrote; "For this reason, I bow my knees to the Father of our Lord Jesus Christ, from whom the whole family in heaven and earth is named, that he would grant you, according to the riches of his glory, to be strengthened with might through his Spirit in the inner man, that Christ may dwell in your hearts through faith; that you, being rooted and grounded in love, may be able to comprehend with all the saints what is the width and length and depth and height – to know the love of Christ which passes knowledge; that you may be filled will all the fullness of God.'

"Now to him who is able to do exceedingly abundantly above all that we ask or think, according to the power that works in us, to him be glory in the church by Christ Jesus throughout all ages, world without end. Amen" (Ephesians 3:14-21).

One can not do anything to reimburse God for the amazing grace he has lavished upon us, we can only show our appreciation, and express our gratitude to him by, the mercies of God to present our bodies a living sacrifice, holy, acceptable to him, which is our reasonable act of worship.

And the reason for this is because as priests of the New

Covenant we are to be holy to our God, because we offer the offerings of the Lord made by fire, and the bread of our God; therefore we shall be holy.

And as obedient children we are not to conform ourselves to the former lusts, as in our ignorance; but as he who called us is holy; we also are to be holy in all our conduct, because it is written, "Be holy, for I am holy."

We should appreciate the fact that, we were not redeemed with corruptible things like silver or gold from our aimless conduct received by tradition from our fathers, but with the precious blood of Christ, as of a lamb without blemish and without spot.

He indeed was foreordained before the foundation of the world, but was manifest in these last times for us who through him believe in God, who raised him from the dead and gave him glory, so that our faith and hope are in God.

A Perfect Sacrifice of Thanksgiving

This is a thanksgiving offering which fulfills the will of the Father. The presenter is urged in view of God's mercy, to present his/her body a living sacrifice, in a holy and acceptable way to the Lord, which is his/her reasonable service, or his/her spiritual act of worship.

This is required of the worshiper in order to offer to the Lord his food for his offering, which gives them the boldness (confidence) to enter the holiest of all in the presence of God. As a matter of fact, the main reason why people come before God to worship is specifically to offer to him his offering.

For thus says the Lord; "These are the Lord's appointed feasts, which you are to proclaim as sacred assemblies for bringing offerings made to the Lord by fire (zeal) – the burnt offerings (Christ the Lamb of God) and grain offerings (Unleavened Bread Christ's body), sacrifices and drink offerings (Wine; Christ's blood) required for each day.

These offerings are besides the Sabbaths of the Lord, besides our gifts, besides all our vows, and besides all our free will offerings which we give to the Lord" (Leviticus 23:37-38).

So important is this offering to God, he instructed Moses saying; "Command the children of Israel and say to them, 'My offering, my food for my offerings made by fire as a sweet aroma to me, you shall be careful to offer to me at their appointed time" (Numbers 28:2).

The Lord said to his disciples, "I am the way, the truth and the life, no one comes to the Father except through me" (John 14:6).

The Way to the Father is the example of life Jesus Christ lived whilst in the flesh, and set us an example that we should follow his steps. This way is the new and living way which he consecrated for us in his flesh.

This way is also figurative to his body, the Church, because in several passages of scripture, the church is referred to as the Way.

For example; Saul before he became the apostle Paul, "Went to the high priest and asked him for letters to the synagogues in Damascus, so that if he found any there who belonged to the Way, whether men or women, he might take them as prisoners to Jerusalem" (Acts 9:2).

When Saul became converted and became known as the apostle Paul, he confessed saying; "I persecuted the followers of this Way to their death, arresting both men and women and throwing them into prison" (Acts.22:4).

On one occasion, "the apostle Paul entered the synagogue and spoke boldly there for three months, arguing persuasively about the kingdom of God, but some of them became obstinate: they refused to believe and publicly maligned the Way.' Also, "About that time, there arose a great disturbance about the Way (Acts 19:9, 23).

The apostle Paul in defending the gospel before Felix said, "However, I admit that I worship the God of our fathers as a follower of the **Way**, which they call a sect." Then Felix, who was well acquainted with the **Way**, adjourned the proceedings" (Acts 24:14, 22).

In several other passages of scripture, the Christian religion is referred to as the **Way** (Acts 9:2; 18:26; 19:9, 23; 22:4; 28:22).

This **Way** is what all believers are called to witness about. The objective of this **Way** is to, "Open the eyes of men [Jews as well as Gentiles] and turn them from darkness to light and from the power of Satan to God, so that they may receive forgiveness of sins and a place among those who are sanctified by faith in Jesus Christ."

We have been called to be a witness to what the apostle Paul saw concerning Jesus Christ and what was revealed to him.

This Way identifies the church, the body of Christ, and distinguishes it from all others. This way is called, "The fellowship of the mystery which from the beginning of the ages has been hidden in God who created all things through Jesus Christ; and the intent was, that now the manifold wisdom of God might be made known by the church to the principalities and powers in the heavenly places, according to the eternal purpose which he accomplished in Christ Jesus our Lord, in whom we have boldness and access with confidence through faith in him" (Ephesians 3:9-12).

This is the wisdom of God in a mystery, the hidden wisdom which God ordained before the ages for our glory, which none of the rulers of this age knew; for had they known, they would not have crucified the Lord of Glory"(1Corinthians 2:7-8).

This is the hidden mystery of the ages which the Lord revealed to the apostle Paul, and he unveiled it to the church at Corinth when he said to them; "For I received from the Lord what I also pass on to you. The Lord Jesus, on the night he was betrayed, took bread, and when he had given thanks, he broke it and said, "This is my body, which is for you: do this in remembrance of me.

"In the same way, after supper he took the cup, saying: 'This cup is the new covenant in my blood: do this, whenever you drink it, in remembrance of me. For whenever you eat this bread and drink this cup, you proclaim the Lord's death until he comes" (1Corinthians 11:23-23-26).

This proclamation is the responsibility of the church to demonstrate to the principalities and powers of the heavenly places, the manifold wisdom of God.

The apostle Paul wrote; "Is not the cup of thanksgiving for which we give thanks a participation in the blood of Christ? And is not the bread that we break a participation in the body of Christ? Because there is one bread: we, who are many, are one body, for, we all partake of the one bread" (1Corinthians 10:16-17).

Therefore, following the example of the life of Jesus Christ, and partaking of his flesh (Unleavened Bread), is the new and living way to the Father

The Truth by which we come to the Father is by the word of God. Jesus said; "Sanctify them by the truth; your word is truth." Jesus Christ is the word of God who became flesh and dwelt amongst us, he is now our High Priest over the house of God, interceding on our behalf. He is the sweet aroma with fulfills the will of God.

The Life by which we come to God is by the blood of Jesus Christ, which is represented by the wine. It is stated quite categorically that, "The life of every creature is in the blood, and God has given it to us to make atonement for our souls on the altar, for it is the blood that makes atonement for the soul" (Leviticus 17:11).

It is for this reason that on the night before Jesus Christ was led to be crucified, he instituted the New Covenant of his blood by blessing the cup and gave thanks saying; "Drink from it, all of you. This is my blood of the covenant, which is poured out for many for the forgiveness of sins" (Matt.26:28).

It is through this process that we can now draw near with a true heart, in full assurance of faith, having our hearts sprinkled from an evil conscience, and our bodies washed with pure water, holding fast the confession of our hope without wavering, for he who promised is faithful. And let us consider one another in order to stir up love and good works, not forsaking the assembling of ourselves together, as the manner of some, but exhorting one another, and so much the more as you see the Day approaching" (Hebrews 10:19-25).

This is our door to the Father, whenever we want to present ourselves before him. For thus says the Lord; "These are the Lord's appointed feasts, which you are to proclaim as sacred assemblies for bringing offerings made to the Lord by fire (zeal) – the burnt offerings (Christ the Lamb of God) and grain offerings (Unleavened Bread Christ's body), sacrifices and drink offerings (Wine; Christ's blood) required for each day.

These offerings are besides the Sabbaths of the Lord, besides our gifts, besides all our vows, and besides all our free will offerings which we give to the Lord" (Leviticus 23:37-38).

This offering is so important to God, he instructed Moses saying; "Command the children of Israel and say to them, 'My offering, my food for my offerings made by fire as a sweet aroma to me, you shall be careful to offer to me at their appointed time" (Numbers 28:2).

The appointed time to offer the Lord his offering is found recorded in the book of Numbers chapter 28 and chapter 29 respectively.

The complexity of man's duality is the choice between living in accordance to the Spirit, which is in accordance to the established laws of God through faith and love, and the choice of living in accordance to the flesh, that of disobedience to the established laws of God, and doing what seems right in one's own eyes, and fulfilling the lustful desires of the flesh.

Chapter Eight

Are we True Witnesses of the Way?

It is quite evident that believers in Jesus Christ are not experiencing the quality of life promised to them in the scriptures. Some are so naive they bear their pains and agony with the pretext that the good, blessed, abundant life promised in scriptures is not for this present age, but for the world to come.

Others believe that they are destined to suffer the same fate and calamities in this world as unbelievers, even though Jesus himself said. "I have come that they [His sheep - believers] may have life and that they may have it more abundantly" (John 10:10).

While others promulgate a false notion of wealth prosperity when Jesus Christ himself warned us saying, "Take heed and beware of covetousness, for one's life does not consists in the abundance of the things he possesses" (Luke 12:15).

The apostle Paul also warned us saying; "Withdraw yourselves from the constant friction between men of corrupt minds, who have been robbed of the truth and who think that godliness is a means to financial gain'; But rather, 'Godliness with contentment is great gain, for we brought nothing into the world, and we can take nothing out of it. But if we have food and clothing, we will be content with that" (1Timothy 6:5-8).

The Apostle Paul endorsed the fact, and proved to us that the abundant life is not related to wealth and prosperity, for he said, "Let your conduct be without covetousness, and be content with such things as you have. For He Himself has said, 'I will never leave you nor forsake you." So we may boldly say: 'The Lord is my helper; I will not fear. What can man do to me?" (Hebrews 13:5-6).

Therefore the way of life to which the believer has been called to be a witness, is not one of despair, self-pity, and sorrow: neither is it that of the prosperity gospel.

Here is what the scriptures say; "Behold, I lay in Zion a chief corner stone, elect, precious, <u>and he who believes on him will by no means be put to shame</u>" (1Peter 2:6).

Those who believe are called, "A Chosen generation, a royal priesthood, a holy nation his own special people." Their witness is to, "<u>Proclaim the praises of him who called them out of darkness into his marvelous light." They also are like living stones being built into a spiritual house to be a holy priesthood, offering spiritual sacrifices acceptable to God through Jesus Christ</u>" (1Peter 2 :9, 5).

It is stated that, "God's divine power has given to them all things that pertain to life and godliness, through the knowledge of him who called them by glory and virtue" (2 Peter 1:3).

Believers are to witness to the world as a holy nation and a royal priesthood. The apostle Paul on his way to Damascus was struck by a light from heaven, which was brighter than the sun, blazing around him and his companions then the Lord said to him, "Now get up and stand on your feet. I have appeared to you to appoint you as a servant and as a witness of what you have seen of me and what I will show you.'

"I will rescue you from your own people and from the Gentiles. I am sending you to them to open their eyes and turn them from darkness to light; and from the power of Satan to God, so that they may receive forgiveness of sins and a place among those who are sanctified by faith in me" (Acts 26:16-18).

Believers are a priestly nation, the church is not a replica of the Jewish religion, neither is it a replica of the Gentile pagan religion. The church is the **Way** that has been consecrated in the flesh of Jesus Christ to grant us bold access to the Father.

What exactly was revealed to the apostle Paul?

What was revealed to the apostle Paul with regards to the **Way** is Jesus Christ, who himself is the **Way** and the truth and the life, and that no one comes to the Father except through him.

What was revealed to the apostle Paul was "The mystery of Christ which in other ages was not made known to the sons of men;' and 'which none of the rulers of this age knew; for had they known, they would not have crucified the Lord of Glory" (Ephesians .3:3-5; 1Corinthians 2:7-8).

The apostle Paul unveiled the mystery to the church at Corinth when he said to them, "For I have received from the Lord what I also passed on to you; The Lord Jesus, on the night he was betrayed, took bread, and when he had given thanks, he broke it and said, "This is my body, which is for you; do this in remembrance of me." In the same way, after supper he took the cup, saying, "This cup is the New Covenant in my blood; do this, whenever you drink it, in remembrance of me." For whenever you eat this bread and drink this cup, you proclaim the Lord's death until he comes" (1Corinthians 1:23-26).

The consummation of this mystery is the trademark of the Christian church. The apostle Paul wrote; "I became a servant of this gospel by the gift of God's grace given me through the working of his power. Although I am less than the least of all God's people, this grace was given me; to preach to the Gentiles the unsearchable riches of Christ, and to make plain to everyone the administration of this mystery, which for ages past was kept hidden in God, who created all things.'

"His intent was that now, through the church, the manifold wisdom of God should be made known to the rulers and authorities in the heavenly realms according to his eternal purpose which he accomplished in Christ Jesus our Lord" (Ephesians 3:7-11).

It is also through the consummation of this mystery and having faith in him, that we may approach God with freedom and confidence. It is at the consummation of this mystery that believers enjoy fellowship with one another and with the Father and his Son Jesus Christ.

It is also at such a fellowship that the sins of the believer are forgiven. Because if we claim to be without sin, we deceive ourselves and the truth is not in us. If we claim we have not sinned, we make him out to be a liar and his word has no place in our lives.

However, "If we confess our sins, he is faithful and just and will forgive us our sins and purify us from all unrighteousness," but, "Without the shedding of blood, there is no remission of sins," therefore, "If we walk in the light, as he is in the light, we have fellowship with one another, and the blood of Jesus, his Son, purifies us from all sin" (1John 1:7-10).

The blood which purifies the believer from sin is the cup of the New Covenant taken at the Lord's Supper. This arrangement was instituted by Jesus Christ on the night before his death, when he took the cup, gave thanks and offered it to the disciples, saying, "Drink from it, all of you. This is my blood of the New Covenant, which is poured out for many for the forgiveness of sins" (Matthew .26:28).

It is through the consummation of this mystery and reaping of its benefits that the believer can truly testify of the **Way**, and, "Give thanks to the Father, who has qualified them to share in the inheritance of the saints in the kingdom of light.

For he has rescued them from the dominion of darkness and brought them into the kingdom of the Son he loves, in whom they have redemption, the forgiveness of sins"(Colossians 1:12-13).

The trademark of the **Way** which is, the fellowship of believers was what really distinguished the first century church. "They devoted themselves to the apostles' teachings and to the fellowship, to the breaking of bread and to prayer.' 'All believers were together and had everything in common" (Acts.2:42).

Indicating that, when they met, they all without exception partook of the bread and wine as confirmed by the apostle Paul who wrote; "So then, my brothers, when you come together to eat, wait for each other. If anyone is hungry, he should eat at home, so that when you meet together it may not result in judgment" (1Corinthians 11:33).

This chosen group has an admonition from the Lord saying, "Do not be yoked together with unbelievers. For what do righteousness and wickedness have in common? Or what fellowship can light have with darkness? What harmony is there between Christ and Belial? What does a believer have in common with an unbeliever? What agreement is there between and temple of God and idols?'

'For we are the temple of the living God, as God has said; I will live with them and walk among them, and I will be their God, and they will be my people.'

'Therefore come out from them and be separate, says the Lord. Touch no unclean thing, and I will receive you. I will be a Father to you, and you will be my sons and daughters, says the Lord Almighty" (2 Corinthians 6:14-18).

Most people equate this warning of not being unequally yoked with unbelievers, more to marriage relationship between a believer, and a non-believer, and to some extent in business relationships. But this warning is even more pronounced in the case where, a believer, in whom the Holy Spirit of God dwells, the future bride of Christ, God's holy temple fellow-shipping together with unbelievers, one in whom the Holy Spirit is not residing, and who has made his/her body an idol of worship.

The Lord spoke to the prophet Ezekiel concerning his people and said, "Her priests do violence to my law and profane my holy things; they do not distinguish between the holy and the common; they teach that there is no difference between the unclean and the clean; and they shut their eyes to the keeping of my Sabbaths, so that I am profaned among them" (Ezekiel 22:26).

Now according to the apostle John; "This is the message we have heard from him [the Way] and declare to you; God is light; in him there is no darkness at all. If we claim to have fellowship with him yet walk in the darkness, we lie and do not live by the truth. But if we walk in the light, as he is in the light, we have fellowship with one another, and the blood of Jesus, his Son, purifies us from all sin" (1John 15-7).

When the church presents itself before God, and partakes of communion; this is figurative to an Old Testament law called the law of jealousy which an unfaithful wife was required to observe to prove her fidelity, as described in the book of Numbers chapter 5 verses 11-29.

This law was applicable when a woman goes astray and defiles herself while married to her husband, or when feelings of jealousy came over a man because he suspected his wife. The priest had her to stand before the Lord and applied the entire law to her. The husband would be innocent of any wrong doing, but the woman would bear the consequences of her sin. If however, the woman had not defiled herself and was free from impurity, she would be cleared of guilt and would be able to have children.

Comparatively, "Whoever eats the bread or drinks the cup of the Lord in an unworthy manner will be guilty of sinning against the body and blood of the Lord. A man ought to examine himself before he eats of the bread and drinks of the cup. For anyone who eats and drinks without recognizing the body of the Lord, eats and drink judgment on him-self. **That is why many among you are weak and sick; and a number of you have fallen asleep.**

This is the epitome of the Christian fellowship; "But if we judged ourselves, we would not come under judgment. When we are judged by the Lord [which takes place at the communion service], we are being disciplined so that we will not be condemned with the world" (1Corinthians 11:31-32).

Therefore, if the church is experiencing the same distress and calamities with the rest of the world, we know the reason why! For we are admonished to, "Come out of her, my people, so that you will not share in her sins, so that you will not receive any of her plagues" (Revelation 18:4).

In conclusion I ask the question again; Are we true witnesses of the **Way**?" Or are we false witnesses!

The Condemnation

In the discussion with Nicodemus regarding the new birth from which the new life in the Spirit originates, Jesus said to him, "And this is the condemnation, that the light has come into the world, and men loved darkness rather than light, because their deeds were evil" (John 3:19).

The light which came in to the world, and was not embraced by the world is the new life in the Spirit, whose kingdom is the Kingdom of Light.

The Kingdom of light similarly to the kingdom of darkness consists of five (5) things (viz.)

1. Territory
2. King
3. Rulers
4. Subjects
5. Laws

1. The Territory

The territory for the kingdom of light is the earth which is now in darkness and is being ruled by Satan and his demonic forces. It is stated that, "The whole world is under the sway of the wicked one" (1John 5:8).

According to Revelation chapter 13 verse 2, "...The dragon (Satan) gave the beast (king or kingdom) his power and his throne and great authority." And men worshiped the dragon because he had given authority to the beast, and they also worshiped the beast and asked, "Who is like the beast? Who can make war with him?"

It further states that; "All inhabitants of the earth will worship the beast...all whose names have not been written in the book of life belonging to the Lamb that was slain from the creation of the world" (Revelation 13: 4, 8).

Because Satan is the ruler of this world, and has given his throne, power, and authority to the beast, and as soon as Jesus Christ who is the heir of the kingdom was born, Satan tried to destroy him.

Jesus came to give life to man and to restore the government of God on earth. When Jesus Christ was born the wise men from the east came to Jerusalem saying, "Where is he who has been born King of the Jews? For we have seen His star in the east and have come to worship Him." When Herod the king who was sitting on the throne of the kingdom of darkness heard these things, he was troubled, and all Jerusalem with him.

Then Herod, when he had secretly called the wise men, determined from them what time the star appeared, and he sent them to Bethlehem and said, "Go and search diligently for the young child, and when you have found him, bring back word to me, that I may come and worship him also" (Matthew 2:1-3).

But when Herod saw that he was deceived by the wise men, he was exceedingly angry; and he sent forth and put to death all the male children who were in Bethlehem and in all its districts, from two years old and under, according to the time which he had determined from the wise men.

But Jesus Christ was not among the dead children, because as soon as the wise men departed, "An angel of the Lord appeared to Joseph in a dream, saying, "Arise, take the young child and his mother, flee to Egypt, and stay there until I bring you word; for Herod will seek the young child to destroy him" (Matthew 2:13).

When Joseph arose from his dream, he took the young child

and his mother by night and departed for Egypt, and was there until the death of Herod.

This was not the only time Satan attempted to take the life of Jesus. He attempted to take his life again at the end of his forty days fasting in the wilderness. He took Jesus to a high mountain and showed him all the kingdoms of the world in a moment of time and said to him, "All this authority I will give you, and their glory; for this has been delivered to me, and I will give it to whomever I wish," Therefore, if you will worship before me, all will be yours" (Luke 4:5-7).

Satan attempted again to destroy the life of Jesus by taking him to Jerusalem and set him on the pinnacle of the temple, and said to him, "If you are the Son of God, throw yourself down from here. For it is written: 'He shall give his angels charge over you, to keep you,' "and in their hands they shall bear you up, lest you dash your feet against a stone" (Luke 4:9-11).

Jesus did not refute Satan's claim as being the ruler of the kingdoms of the earth, instead he said to his disciples, "I will not speak with you much longer, for the prince [ruler] of this world is coming. He has no hold on me, but the world must learn that I love the Father and that I do exactly what my Father has commanded me, come now; let us leave" (John.14:30-31).

Jesus Christ who is the heir and ruler of the earth came to his own (territory) and his own (people) did not receive him. In the parable of the wicked Vine-dresser it is clearly stated that the vineyard [earth] has been leased to vine-dressers, who have repeatedly beaten, ill-treated, and shamefully sent away empty-handed, all servants sent by the owner of the vineyard to receive some fruit from the vineyard during vintage time.

Then the owner of the vineyard said, "What shall I do? I will send my beloved son. Probably they will respect him when they see him.' "But when the vine-dressers saw him, they reasoned among themselves, saying, 'This is the heir. Come, let us kill him, that the inheritance may be ours,' "So they cast him out of the vineyard and killed him. Therefore what will the owner of the vineyard do to them?'

"He will come and destroy those vine-dressers and give the vineyard to others" (Luke .20:13-16).

The world has been under the control of four (4) successive world powers, prophetically known as the four (4) Beasts. Namely:-

1. The Chaldean or Babylonian Empire

2. The Persian Empire

3. Grecian-Macedonian Empire

4. The Roman Empire

According to the Prophet Daniel, "Those great beasts, which are four, are four kings [kingdoms] which arise out of the earth. But the saints of the Most shall receive the kingdom, and possess the kingdom forever, even forever and ever" (Dan.2:36-45; 7:17-18).

2. King

The kingdom of light is ruled and governed by the King and His Co-heirs. The king of the kingdom of light is Jesus Christ and His kingship began from birth, as it is written; "For unto us a child is born, unto us a Son is given; and the government will be upon his shoulder. And his name will be called Wonderful, Counselor, mighty God, Everlasting Father, prince of peace.'

"Of the increase of his government and peace there will be no end, upon the throne of David and over his kingdom, to order it and establish it with judgment and justice from that time forward, even forever. The zeal of the Lord of hosts will perform this" (Isaiah 9:6-7).

The wise men from the East who saw the star, and traveled to Jerusalem to visit the Lord, on entering Jerusalem they asked, "Where is he who has been born King of the Jews? For we have seen his star in the East and have come to worship him." (Matthew 2:11).

When they met him as a young child with his parents in a house, they fell down and worshiped him, and presented him gifts; gold in honor of a king; frankincense in honor of his divinity as God; and myrrh in honor of his humanness as man

The Pharisees asked Jesus, "When will the kingdom of God come? He answered them and said, "The kingdom of God does not come with observation; nor will they say, 'see here!' Or 'See there!' For indeed, the kingdom of God is within you [in your midst]" (Luke 20:21).

When asked by Pilate during his trial, "Are you the King of the Jews? Jesus answered him, "Are you speaking for yourself on this, or did others tell you this about me?' Pilate answered, "Am I a Jew? Your own nation and the chief priests have delivered you to me. What have you done?' Jesus answered, "My kingdom is not of this world. If my kingdom were of this world, my servants would fight, so that I should not be delivered to the Jews; but now my kingdom is not from here."

Pilate therefore said to him, "Are you a King then? Jesus answered, "You say rightly that I am a King. For this cause, I was born and for this cause, I have come into the world, that I should bear witness to the truth. Everyone who is of the truth hears my voice" (John.18:35-37).

The birth of Jesus Christ inaugurated the kingdom of light on earth. He was the [representative of the] kingdom of God that was in the midst of the people. Every fifteenth day of the seventh month according to the Jewish sacred calendar, a feast called The Feast of Tabernacles is celebrated in honor of the King, and the Lord of hosts.

This festival falls on the full moon during the end of September, or early October and commemorates the birth of Jesus Christ. On the Eighth day of this festival, another festival is celebrated commemorating the circumcision of Jesus Christ.

Jesus Christ who is the King of the kingdom of light, made no attempt to support or be part of the kingdom of darkness. During one Passover season after Jesus Christ fed five thousand people with five barley loaves and two small fishes, some people when they saw the sign that he did, said, "This is truly the prophet who is to come into the world." Therefore when Jesus perceived that they were about to come and take him by force to make him king he departed again to a mountain by himself alone" (John.6: 14-15).

3 Rulers

The Rulers of the kingdom of light are joint heirs of God and joint heirs with Christ. They are those who have received Him [the light - the life], and were given the right or authority to become children of God, even to those who believe in His name.

They are to give thanks to the Father who has qualified them to be partakers of the inheritance of the saints in the light. Because: He has delivered them from the power of darkness and translated them into the kingdom of the Son of his love.

The joint heirs of the kingdom of light have been called out of this world. Jesus said to his disciples, "If the world hates you, you know that it hated me before it hated you. If you were of the world, the world would love its own. Yet because you are not of the world, but I chose you out of the world, therefore the world hates you" (John.15:18-19).

In praying for his disciples Jesus said, "I pray for them. I do not pray for the world but for those whom you have given me, for they are yours and all mine are yours, and yours are mine, and I am glorified in them. Now I am no longer in the world, but these are in the world, and I come to you.'

"Holy Father, keep through your name those whom you have given me, that they may be one as we are, but now I come to you, and these things I speak in the world, that they may have my joy fulfilled in themselves. I have given them your word; and the world has hated them because they are not of the world, just as I am not of the world.

I do not pray that you should take them out of the world, but that you should keep them from the evil one. They are not of the world, just as I am not of the world. Sanctify them by your truth. Your word is truth. As you sent me into the world, I also have sent them into the world" (John.17:9-11, 13-18).

Jesus Christ was sent into the world to draw people to himself from both Jews and Gentiles who were in bondage in the kingdom of darkness. He has created in himself one new man from the two, so that He might reconcile them both to God in one body through the cross, thereby putting to death the enmity which existed between them.

Christ's disciples are required to follow his example by drawing both Jews and Gentiles away from the kingdom of darkness and be translated into the kingdom of light.

The joint heirs of the kingdom of light have received the heavenly calling to, "Come out of her my people, lest you share in her sins, and lest you receive of her plagues" (Revelation 18:4). They have also received a warning saying,

"Adulterers and adulteresses! Do you not know that friendship with this world is enmity with God? Whoever therefore wants to be a friend of the world makes himself an enemy of God" (James 4:4).

The joint heirs of the kingdom of light are sojourners and pilgrims. "They are to abstain themselves from fleshly lusts which war against the soul. They are to submit themselves to every ordinance of man for the Lord's sake, whether to the king as supreme, or to governors, as to those who are sent by him [the king] for the punishment of evildoers and for the praise of those who are good.'

"For this the will of God, that by doing good you may put to silence the ignorance of foolish men.' "They are to honor all people, love the brotherhood. Fear God. Honor the king" (1Peter 2:11-17).

The joint heirs of the kingdom of light should not make the mistake of equating the dispensation of the kingdom of light, which was inaugurated at the birth of Jesus Christ, with the time of Joseph and Daniel when only the kingdom of darkness was in authority. They must never forget Jesus' statement saying, "I have given them you word; and the world has hated them because they are not of the world, just as I am not of the world. I do not pray that you should take them out of the world, but that you should keep them from the evil one. They are not of the world, just as I am not of the world" (John 17:14-16).

One must not forget that, "When Jesus Christ perceived that they were about to come and take Him by force to make him king, he departed again to a mountain by himself alone" (John 6:15). And he said to Pilate "My kingdom is not of this world. If my kingdom were of this world, my servants would fight, so that I should not be delivered to the Jews; but now my kingdom is not from here" (John.18:36).

Now the children of light who abides in Jesus Christ, ought themselves to walk just as he walked, and, "Love has been perfected among us in this: that we may have boldness in the Day of Judgment; because as he is, so are we in this world" (1John 2:6; 1John 4:17).

The heirs of God and joint heirs with Christ: are those who have indeed suffered with Christ similarly to how He himself suffered in the flesh. It is stated that "Jesus Christ had to be made like his brethren, in order that he might be a merciful and faithful High Priest in things pertaining to God, to make propitiation for the sins of the people, for in that He Himself has suffered, being tempted, He is able to aid those who are tempted." And therefore, "Since Christ suffered for us in the flesh, we are to arm ourselves also with the same mind, for he who has suffered in the flesh has ceased from sin" (Hebrews 2:17-18; 1Peter 4:1).

The Rulers and joint heirs of the kingdom will rule and reign with Christ during his Millennial reign on earth. These joint-heirs were redeemed out of every tribe and tongue and people and nation, and they have made a kingdom of priests to our God; and they shall reign on the earth.

In the new heaven and the new earth, they will form part of the New Jerusalem. The Twelve gates of the city: three on the east, three on the north, three on the south, and three on the west represent the one hundred and forty- four thousand of all the tribes of the children of Israel.

The twelve foundations represent the twelve Apostles of the Lamb; and the walls built on the twelve foundations are the joint heirs who as living stones, are being built up a spiritual house, a holy priesthood, to offer up spiritual sacrifices acceptable to God through Jesus Christ. "They have been built on the foundation of the apostles and prophets, Jesus Christ himself being the chief cornerstone, in whom the whole building being joined together, grows into a holy temple in the Lord, in whom you also are being built together for a habitation of God in the Spirit"(Revelation 21:12-16; 1Peter 2:5;Ephesians 2:20-22).

The call of duty for the Co-heirs of the kingdom of light, whilst sojourning in the kingdom of darkness, is learning how to be shrewd [cleverness in practical affairs], using worldly wealth [mammon] to gain friends for themselves, so that when it is gone, they will be welcomed into everlasting habitations.'

Because, 'whoever can be trusted with very little can also be trusted with much, and whoever is dishonest with very little will also be dishonest with much. So if you have not been trustworthy in handling worldly wealth: who will trust you with true riches? And, if you have not been trustworthy in that which belongs to another: who will give you property of your own? (Luke.16:9-12).

No matter how much one might possess in the kingdom of darkness, it is least in comparison to what is attainable in the kingdom of light. Therefore; "Let us not lay up for ourselves treasures on earth, where moth and rust destroy and where thieves break in and steal; but let us lay up for ourselves treasures in heaven, where neither moth nor rust destroys and where thieves do not break in and steal. For where our treasure is, there our heart will be also" (Matthew 6:19-21).

4. Subjects

The subjects of the kingdom of light are those who are saved out of all the nations of the earth. "They shall walk in its light, and the kings of the earth shall bring their glory and honor unto it. The gates of the city shall not be shut at all by day [there shall be no night there]. And the subjects shall bring the glory and the honor of the nations into it.'

"But there shall by no means enter it anything that defiles, or causes an abomination or a lie, but only those who are written in the Lamb's Book of Life" (Revelation 21:24-27)

They will have access to the tree of life which will bear twelve fruits, each tree yielding its fruit every month. And the leaves of the tree will be for the healing of the nations.

There shall be no more curses, but the throne of God and of the Lamb shall be in it, and his servants shall serve him. They will have access to the water of life, and the Spirit and the bride will say, "Come!" And let him who hears say, "Come!" And let him who thirst come. And whoever desires let him take the water of life freely"

The subjects unlike the joint-heirs and joint-rulers with Christ, will be void of immortality, and will have to partake of the tree of life and of the living water in order for their lives to be perpetuated, and the leaves of the tree of life for their healing.

5. LAWS

The kingdom of light is not a lawless kingdom. It is established on laws and principles. To the Begotten Son, the ruler of the kingdom of light God said, "Your throne, O God, is forever and ever; a scepter of righteousness is the scepter of your kingdom. You have loved righteousness and hated lawlessness; therefore God, your God, has anointed you with the oil of gladness more than your companions" (Psalms 45:6-7; Hebrews 1:8-9).

The Prophet Micah prophesied about the kingdom of God saying; "Now it shall come to pass in the latter days that the mountain [kingdom] of the Lord's house shall be established on the top of the mountains [kingdoms], and shall be exalted above the hills; and peoples shall flow to it. Many nations shall come and say, "Come, and let us go up to the mountain [kingdom] of the Lord, to the house of the God of Jacob; He will teach us his ways, and we shall walk in his paths." 'For out of Zion the law shall go forth, and the word of the Lord from Jerusalem" (Micah 4:1-2).

The kingdom of darkness in contrast to the kingdom of light is a lawless kingdom because its subjects have rejected the laws by which mankind should live, and every man choose what seems right in his/her own eyes. There is only one law by which man should live.

And this one law or way of life, God has revealed it to only one nation, the children of Israel. The one who instructed the children of Israel in the wilderness and wrote the Ten Commandments with his own fingers: is the same one who became the begotten Son of God, and who will rule this earth forever and ever.

When he came to the world this is what he said, "Do not think that I came to destroy the law or the Prophets. I did not come to destroy but to fulfill. For assuredly, I say to you, till heaven and earth pass away, one jot or one tittle will by no means pass from the law till all is fulfilled.'

"Whoever therefore breaks one of the least of these commandments, and teaches men so, shall be called least in the kingdom of heaven; but whoever does and teaches them, he shall be called great in the kingdom of heaven" (Matthew 5:17-19).

Both Moses [the law} and the Prophets received instructions from God as to how man should live. The Lord spoke to Moses saying, "Speak to the children of Israel and say to them: I am the Lord your God." 'You shall observe my judgments and keep my ordinances, to walk in them: I am the Lord your God. You shall therefore keep my statutes and my judgments, which if a man does, he shall live by them: I am the Lord" (Leviticus 18:4-5).

The Lord also spoke to Ezekiel the prophet saying, "I made

them go out of the land of Egypt and brought them into the wilderness, and I gave them my statutes and showed them my judgments, <u>which, if a man does, he shall live by them..</u>'

"Moreover I also gave them My Sabbaths, to be a sign between them and me that they might know that I am the Lord who sanctifies them. Yet the house of Israel rebelled against me in the wilderness; they did not walk in my statutes; they despised my judgments<u>, which, if a man does, he shall live by them;</u> and they greatly defiled my Sabbaths. Then I said I would pour out my fury on them in the wilderness, to consume them" (Ezekiel 20:11-13).

In the parable of the rich man and Lazarus we have an illustration where the rich man being in torment begged Abraham to send Lazarus to his father's house where he the rich man had five brothers, that Lazarus may testify to them, lest they also come to this place of torment.

But Abraham said to him. "They have Moses and the Prophets; let them hear them.' And he [the rich man] said, 'No, father Abraham; but if one goes to them from the dead, they will repent.' 'But he [Abraham] said to him, 'If they do not hear Moses and the prophets, neither will they be persuaded though one rise from the dead" (Luke 16:27-31).

There is only one way which, if a man does, he shall live by them, and this is the one both Moses and the prophets spoke about. The Lord spoke to Moses saying, "All who are native born shall do these things in this manner, in presenting an offering made by fire, a sweet aroma to the Lord. And if a stranger sojourns with you, or whoever is among you throughout your generations, and would present an offering made by fire, a sweet aroma to the Lord, just as you do, so shall he do.'

<u>"One ordinance shall be for you of the congregation and for the stranger who sojourns with you, an ordinance forever</u>

<u>throughout your generation; as you are, so shall the stranger be before the Lord. One law and one custom shall be for you and for the stranger who sojourns with you"</u> (Numbers15:13-16)

To anyone who might take offense with "Presenting an offering made by fire, a sweet aroma to the Lord:" this sweet aroma is the presentation of the body and blood of Jesus Christ, through the ordinance of communion.

Co-heirs of the kingdom of light are to be followers of God as dear children. And are to walk in love, as Christ also has loved us and given Himself for us, an offering and a sacrifice to God for a sweet-smelling aroma" (Ephesians 5:2).

This age in which we now live, is evil. It is in subjection to [fallen] angels. Our struggles are not against flesh and blood, but against principalities, against powers, against the rulers of the darkness of this age [kingdom of darkness], against spiritual hosts of wickedness in the heavenly places, and, "Although we walk in the flesh, we do not war according to the flesh. For the weapons of our warfare are not carnal but mighty in God for pulling down strong holds" (2 Corinthians10:3-4).

Jesus Christ gave Himself for our sins, so that he might deliver us from this present evil age, according to the will of our God and Father.

Unfortunately, the verdict is, "Light has come into the world, but men love darkness rather than light, because their deeds are evil. For everyone practicing evil hates the light, and does not come to the light, lest his deeds should be exposed. But he who does the truth comes to the light. That his deeds may be clearly seen, that they have been done in God" (John 3:19-21).

Let us strive to avoid being under condemnation, because it is only those who are in Christ Jesus, and who do not walk according to the flesh, and are walking according to the Spirit that are under no condemnation, but those who love the kingdom of darkness rather than the kingdom of light and are walking in accordance to the flesh are under condemnation.

Summary

In the pages of this book I have looked at Man's Duality, a reality which most people have not yet come to terms with, and with little or no knowledge of.

Chapter one seeks to explain the reality of a life which exists in the flesh and one which exists in the spirit. A man who is outward and one who is inward: a mind which is carnal and desperately wicked, and one which is spiritual, law abiding and righteous.

Chapter two shows the process by which both the outward man and the inward man grows and develop simultaneously, and while the outward man is perishing and results in corruption and death, the inward man on the other hand, is renewed day by day, and the end result is everlasting life.

Chapter three shows the constant struggle which goes on between the flesh and the spirit, thus inhibiting the individual from doing the things that he/she wishes: and the wrestle which goes on against principalities, against powers, against the world rulers of this present darkness, and against spiritual hosts of wickedness in the heavenly places. It shows the nature of this warfare, and the role which angels play in human lives.

Chapter four explains the power of choice, for we have all been given the prerogative to choose whether to live in accordance to the flesh, or to live in accordance to the spirit, it discloses what is man's greatest challenge, and how to aspire to become faithful and productive servants.

Chapter five explains the one hope which belongs to our calling, and that there is absolutely no excuse, because there is only one foundation on which we are to build our eternal home.

Chapter six explains our freedom from sin, and how we

should learn to put our trust in God, and what is expected of us if indeed we have proved the Lord is gracious.

Chapter seven looks at the Chief Corner Stone chosen and precious, and he who believe in him will not be put to shame, but to those who do not believe, the very stone which the builders rejected has become the head of the corner stone, and a stone that will make men stumble, a rock that will make them fall, for they stumble because they disobey the word, as they were destined to do. It deals also with the mystery of God's will, which none of the rulers of this age understood, for had they known, they would not have crucified the Lord of glory, and how it became a perfect sacrifice of thanksgiving.

Chapter eight concludes the book with a close examination as to whether we are true witnesses of the Way, the way of the Spirit, and how God did not send his Son into the world to condemn it but that the world might be saved through him. Any condemnation therefore is because the light has come into the world, and men loved darkness rather than light, because their deeds were evil. The darkness is figurative to the life in the flesh, and the light is figurative to the life in the Spirit.

If we know these things happy are we if we do them, we should all endeavor to build on the eternal foundation which Jesus Christ has established for us, our eternal home to the praise and glory of God.

Lucius Joseph